WEAVING TEXTILES
THAT SHAPE THEMSELVES

Ann Richards

WEAVING TEXTILES
THAT SHAPE THEMSELVES

Ann Richards

THE CROWOOD PRESS

First published in 2012 by
The Crowood Press Ltd
Ramsbury, Marlborough
Wiltshire SN8 2HR

www.crowood.com

This impression 2016

British Library Cataloguing-in-Publication Data
A catalogue record for this book is available from the British Library.

ISBN 978 1 84797 319 1

Cover illustration: 'Gauze Pleat' scarf. Tussah silk and mohair.

Frontispiece: 'Dragonfly Pleat' scarf. Linen and silk.

Dedication
To my mother.

Typeset by Sara Millington
Printed and bound in India by Replika Press Pvt. Ltd.

CONTENTS

ACKNOWLEDGEMENTS

I would like to thank all the teachers, friends and colleagues who developed my interest in this field – especially Mary Restieaux, who encouraged me to apply to study at West Surrey College of Art and Design (Farnham), Margaret Bide, who accepted me as a student (and has worked tirelessly to ensure that high-twist woollen yarns remain available for handweavers), and Amelia Uden and Deryn O'Connor, who were my stimulating and supportive tutors at college. I am conscious also of the influence of the late Ella McLeod, though I met her only briefly, since she founded the weaving department at Farnham and was responsible for establishing its unique ethos. I am also grateful to the late Marianne Straub, who came as a visiting tutor and gave me a great deal of encouragement.

Junichi Arai has, of course, been an important influence and inspiration, and I am very glad that he has allowed me to include some of his work in my book. Reiko Sudo, the other founder of Nuno, also kindly agreed to my including her work and other Nuno fabrics. Ann Sutton, who first introduced me to the work of Junichi Arai and Nuno, has been an ongoing source of encouragement and, as well as allowing me to include a piece of her own work, generously allowed me to borrow textiles from her collection for photography. Inge Cordsen and Kate Crosfield, of Livingstone Studio, have been a great source of help and advice, as well as selling my work over many years.

I would also like to thank all the other designers and artists who have allowed me to include examples of their work in this book: Sharon Alderman, Dörte Behn, Anna Champeney, Fiona Crestani, Lotte Dalgaard, Alison Ellen, Berthe Forchhammer, Mary Frame, Stacey Harvey-Brown, Teresa Kennard, Bobbie Kociejowski, Gilian Little, Noriko Matsumoto, Wendy Morris, Andreas Möller, Jennie Parry, Geraldine St Aubyn Hubbard, Ann Schmidt-Christensen, Lucia Schwalenberg, Emma Sewell, Liz Williamson and Deirdre Wood. All textiles not otherwise attributed are by me.

There are two good friends whom, sadly, I am unable to thank personally as they are no longer alive, but I am very glad that family members were happy for me to use examples of their work here. I am grateful to Brian Austin for permission to include a piece by Gusti Austin Lina, and to Peter Reimann for allowing me to include work by Sheila Reimann.

Photographs have been taken by the designers and artists themselves and also by Ole Akhøj, Joe Coca, Alan Costall, Ian Hobbs, Jürgen Liefmann, Joe Low, Colin Mills, Heiko Preller and Carol Sawyer. Other photographs are by the author.

I would especially like to thank Alan Costall for help and advice while I was writing this book.

INTRODUCTION:
Woven Textiles as Self-Organizing Structures

The structure of a fabric or its weave – that is, the fastening of its elements of threads to each other – is as much a determining factor in its function as is the choice of the raw material. In fact, the interrelation of the two, the subtle play between them in supporting, impeding, or modifying each other's characteristics, is the essence of weaving.

Anni Albers, 1965

In some ways, the title of this book is, of course, meant to be playful and a little provocative. Designing and weaving textiles is hard work. Why do I want to say they can 'shape themselves'?

It makes sense to talk about 'self-organization' in designed structures because good design is not merely the *imposition* of form, but depends also on what materials and structures can do. Although the designer can start with a specific aim in view and choose what elements to put together, the materials and the structure will determine what happens, sometimes in surprising ways. Through complex interactions, these elements may organize themselves into something rather different from the intended design. This can perhaps give a

'Doublecloth Loop' scarf, in spun silk and crepe wool, designed to be interlaced around the neck in a variety of different ways. The crepe wool weft gives a textured surface to the scarf, and changes in weave structure create flared borders.

disappointing result but it may also, sometimes, produce something more subtle and interesting than the designer's first thought. Even an apparent failure can form the germ of a new idea. So it is necessary to be constantly attentive to this 'subtle play' of material and structure and be ready to respond, making best use of their characteristics. The design process must be a series of experiments, with the designer reflecting carefully upon each result and trying to understand what is happening before deciding on the next step.

Complex interactions of this sort are characteristic of all designing that is pursued through the process of making, no matter what the material, wood, clay or metal. But woven textiles show this 'self-organizing' tendency to a striking degree, especially if very strong contrasts of material and structure are used. Powerful textures can emerge during wet finishing, from the interplay of fibre, yarn twist and weave structure. Such fabrics undergo a surprising transformation from the smooth, flat state that they have on the loom, to the textured surfaces they develop when they have been soaked in water. As water is absorbed, yarns of differing elasticity pull against one another and ripple or buckle the fabric.

The most dramatic effects are produced by yarns that are very highly twisted and these form the main focus of this book. High-twist yarns can create striking, three-dimensional effects, because the stress imposed by the spinning process gives these yarns considerable energy, which is released by the addition of water. Spontaneous shrinking and spiralling movements of the yarns then cause the fabric to crinkle or pleat, creating highly textured, elastic fabrics. It is also possible to vary the yarn twist or weave structure in different areas of the fabric, resulting in differing amounts of contraction, so that rectangular pieces of fabric assume flared, curved or irregular lozenge shapes when they are wet finished. These textiles can truly shape themselves.

The book begins with an introduction to the physical properties of different textile fibres, the structure of yarns and the influence of yarn twist on the properties of yarns and fabrics, since these factors form the basis of design in woven textiles. Chapter 2 aims to give some historical context, since some techniques go back thousands of years. Chapter 3 deals with yarn counts and how these can be used for calculations of yarn diameter, cloth setting and twist angle, which provide a sound basis for weave design in general, but are particularly useful when working with high-twist yarns.

The next four chapters cover the use of various weave structures that work well with high-twist yarns and contrasting materials. This section is not intended to give an exhaustive treatment of different weave structures, since many excellent books on this topic are already available. Rather the aim is to draw attention to fundamental characteristics and properties of different *groups of structures*, showing their potential for creating textured fabrics.

Chapter 8 deals with practical techniques for handling high-twist and difficult yarns. This is followed by a short chapter, which briefly touches on some topics related to the main theme: the use of synthetic shrinking yarns, other methods of creating textured effects and shaping, and the use of high-twist and shrinking yarns with textile techniques other than weaving.

The concluding chapter discusses sampling, building on experience and the idea of design as 'reflective practice'. When working with powerful yarn twists, the unpredictability of the interactions means that apparently modest changes to any of the elements can create major repercussions within the fabric. So although there are many examples throughout the book (some with details of yarns and cloth settings), there are no projects in the form of detailed 'recipes' that are intended to be followed exactly, since any departure from precise specifications could considerably change the result. The availability of particular yarns is always variable, so it is much better to understand general principles on which personal experience can be built. However, the final chapter includes some suggestions for sampling that I hope will be helpful as a starting point for anyone who has not worked with these yarns before.

Although high-twist yarns and strongly textured textiles form the main focus of the book, I hope that much of the information on both technique and design may be useful to weavers generally. I have included illustrations of textiles by many designers and artists, and have referred in the text and bibliography to other weavers who are doing impressive work in this field. So I hope this book will also serve as a celebration of the variety and beauty of the textiles being produced in this most exuberant area of weave design.

OPPOSITE:
Wool and silk crepe yarns are played off against stiff metal yarns, to create close-fitting bracelets with rippled edges.

CHAPTER 1

FIBRES, YARNS AND WEAVE STRUCTURES

A deep, intuitive appreciation of the inherent cussedness of materials and structures is one of the most valuable accomplishments an engineer can have. No purely intellectual quality is really a substitute for this.

Gordon, *Structures*, 1978

Replace the word 'engineer' with 'designer' in this quotation from Gordon's excellent book *Structures*, and you have a good description of a successful designer/maker. There is no substitute for *working* with materials and processes to develop a deep, intuitive sense that goes beyond theoretical knowledge. Technical specifications of the properties of materials and structures are inevitably measured on the basis of 'other things being equal'. In the real situation of designing, of course, other things never are equal – everything is going on at once! This complexity can sometimes seem unmanageable. And it is here that an intuitive sense of the 'cussedness of materials and structures' really pays off.

All the same, it is well worth knowing something about the scientific measurements of the properties of different materials and structures. This forms a useful base on which to build the 'tacit knowledge' that can only be acquired through practical work. This chapter deals with some basic characteristics of fibres, yarns and weave structures and the way these affect the finished fabric. Although this involves going into

A fabric that spontaneously pleats itself is shown in the loomstate (top) and after wet finishing. I was a beginner in weaving when I first became aware of this effect, while trying to make a fabric with a smooth, flat surface. At the time, I was not too pleased. Later, I came to appreciate the way the cussedness of materials and structures can sometimes be a gift to the designer!

apparently dry technical details, it is worth understanding these basic principles, because so much of the work of making textured textiles relies on subtle differences of material and structure. Also, in the process of examining these various properties separately, the difficulties of designing become apparent. Time and again, it is the *interplay* of properties that is important.

The Properties of Textile Fibres

Although a very wide range of materials can be used to make textiles, the vast majority of all textiles made from natural materials are in cotton, flax, silk or wool. So I want to look at some properties of these common materials that are particularly relevant to their use in textiles.

Strength

One of the most important properties is strength. Scientifically, this is measured by seeing how much weight a sample of the material can support before it breaks, and such tests show that flax is a very strong fibre, while silk and cotton are of moderate strength and wool is very much weaker. Weavers tend to check the strength of yarns by pulling on them to see how easily they break, which is clearly a rough and ready equivalent of the scientific test, and gives similar results. (This is not, of course, strictly comparable with the scientific test, which is done on a sample of the *fibre* itself. As weavers, we are doing our test on a structure – the *yarn*. The structure imposed by the spinning process also influences the strength of the yarn.)

Toughness

But, of course, some of the problems that arise in weaving are not really about strength as such. For example, although linen yarns are strong in the sense that they seem hard to break deliberately, they actually break more easily during weaving than silk, cotton and wool yarns, which are not as 'strong'. The issue here is *toughness*, the ability of a material to absorb energy without breaking. Silk is much the toughest of the natural fibres, with wool and cotton much less so, while flax is relatively brittle. A small amount of damage to a flax fibre easily starts a crack that runs rapidly right through the fibre and causes it to break. This ties in with the experience that linen yarns are easily damaged by the heddles and reed. A simple test for abrasion resistance is to hold a short length of yarn under tension and run a fingernail back and forth along it. It can be surprising to see how an apparently 'strong' linen yarn will sometimes break easily under this treatment. Also a shuttle hitting a linen end stuck in the middle of the shed will often snap the yarn, when a silk yarn would simply absorb the blow. In this case, it is not really the *suddenness* of the force that is the main problem, but the amount of energy the shuttle has as it flies through the shed. It not only starts cracks but also has the energy to propagate them rapidly through the material.

Stiffness

There are also often tension problems with linen yarns because flax is a very *stiff* fibre, compared with silk, cotton and wool. These differences can easily be sensed when handling yarns in these different materials. The flexibility of the wool can readily be felt and seen, as it is easily extensible, and it also shows good elastic recovery, springing back to its original length. Cotton and silk seem moderately flexible, and flax is very inflexible. Many of the weaving difficulties associated with linen yarns are due to the extreme stiffness of the flax fibre. Any slight differences in the tension of individual warp ends makes weaving difficult, compared with a wool yarn that would easily absorb these variations. Also, flax only shows elastic recovery over a small range of stresses. Beyond this point it will not spring back to its former length, so any individual threads in a warp that are accidentally stretched will become slack and interfere with weaving.

Fibre Properties in Textured Textiles

It is clear that strength and toughness are the most important properties of textile fibres, in terms of their general suitability for weaving, especially as warp yarns that must withstand both tension and abrasion. However, from the point of view of designing strongly textured textiles, the *stiffness* of fibres is particularly interesting. At first sight, the fact that linen is so stiff seems to mark it out as difficult to work with, and it is certainly often described as 'unforgiving'. But, quite apart from the fact that linen is a very beautiful material and well worth the extra effort needed in handling it, it is very useful when designing textured textiles. The extreme contrast between the stiffness of linen and the flexibility of the other natural fibres gives plenty of scope for playing these different qualities off against one another to create textured effects.

Variations in fibre stiffness also mean that the properties of high-twist yarns vary, depending on the material. Twisting fibres into yarns imposes a stress on them, and this is the cause of the texture produced by high-twist yarns. Stiff materials that resist twisting react strongly to stress and so can make particularly effective high-twist yarns. The mechanism of this stress reaction will be discussed in more detail later in this chapter. Stiffness is determined not only by the intrinsic differences, for example between such fibres as cotton, silk and wool, but also the thickness of the fibres. The stiffness of a fibre increases more rapidly than its diameter, and consequently wool, with its wide range of fibre diameters found in different breeds of sheep, is a particularly interesting material for high-twist yarns. Different reactions are given by woollen yarns constructed from fine fibres, and worsted yarns made from thicker longwools. The impact of these differences will be explored in Chapter 4.

Structure of Yarns

When, as weavers, we carry out informal tests of the physical properties of our materials by breaking yarns and so on, we are confounding the properties of the fibres themselves and that of the structures made from them – the yarns. The structure of yarns varies and can considerably modify the properties of the fibres.

This fabric uses the effect of soft pleating shown at the beginning of this chapter, but now the pleats also have a rippled effect, because of the contrast between stiff linen yarns and more flexible silk ones.

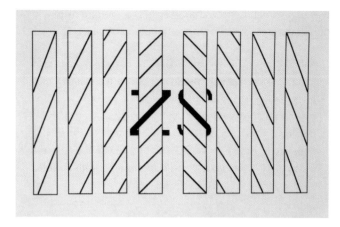

Yarns can be twisted in two different directions (Z and S) and they can also be twisted by different amounts to give varying angles of twist.

An unbalanced yarn will twist back on itself to make a plied yarn.

Yarns may either be formed of continuous filaments or spun from shorter fibres. Continuous filaments, such as silk, do not require twist to give them strength, though they are usually lightly twisted to make a yarn that is more coherent. Yarns made from short fibres, such as wool, cotton or linen, *must* be twisted in order to form a yarn of sufficient strength for weaving. Yarns may be twisted either to the left or the right and these different directions are indicated by the letters S and Z, the diagonal strokes of these two letters lying in line with the fibres in the yarn. A yarn may also be twisted by different amounts and, as more twist is added, the fibres within the yarn will be seen to form a progressively larger angle with the axis of the yarn.

This *twist angle* is an important fundamental property of the yarn, which is covered in more detail in chapter 3. In general, the strength of spun yarns increases with the amount of twist, and this effect is familiar to anyone who spins their own yarn. At very low twists the fibres are free to slip past one another, causing the yarn to break. As twist is increased, the fibre slippage is reduced and the yarn becomes stronger. However, strength increases only up to a certain limit. Beyond this point, further twist imposes a progressively increasing stress, which weakens the yarn. Consequently, there will be an optimum amount of twist to give maximum strength for any particular fibre, depending on such characteristics as length, fineness, smoothness and stiffness. Yarns spun to this optimum twist will generally be rather hard, so for many purposes yarns are spun to a twist angle below the optimum for strength.

Stress and the Creping Reaction

The stress produced by high levels of twist has an additional effect. Yarns become *unbalanced*, tending to crinkle and spiral in an attempt to escape the stress imposed on them, and it is these movements that create textured 'crepe' effects within a woven fabric. Although some fibres produce yarns that react in this way at fairly modest levels of twist, most yarns will need to be spun to higher than the optimum twist required for strength, if they are to have good creping properties (commercial crepe yarns will be well above this optimum). High-twist yarns are therefore usually weaker than normal yarns.

If allowed to, an unbalanced yarn will readily fold back upon itself, forming a double strand twisted in the opposite direction to its initial twist. As this occurs, the single strands are untwisting, allowing the fibres to lie at a lower angle with the axis of the yarn, thus reducing stress and producing a *balanced* yarn, which shows no tendency to crinkle or spiral. This reaction is the basis for the process of combining two or more strands of a *singles* yarn to create a *plied* (or *folded*) yarn. The letters S and Z are used to indicate plying direction in a similar way as for singles yarns.

Direction of Twist

Unlike the amount of twist, the different *directions* of twist do not influence the physical properties of the yarn, such as strength, but Z and S yarns do reflect light in different directions and so can produce subtle 'shadow' stripes and checks when the yarns are woven (*see* Chapter 2). Also, as the warp and weft interlace, different fabric characteristics develop, in terms of handle and surface texture, depending on whether these yarns are both of the same twist (Z × Z or S × S) or have different twists (Z × S). Textural differences are particularly strong with high-twist yarns, and this will be covered in detail in Chapter 4.

Fibre Alignment

A further variation in yarn structure is the extent to which fibres are aligned along the length of a yarn. This greatly affects its properties, so that different preparation and spinning methods can result in very different yarns, even when using the same fibre. But since the fibres themselves also vary in their inherent properties, the interplay between fibre and yarn structure produces a wide variety of yarn qualities. Yarns that are strongly aligned have a smoother surface than those that are less strongly aligned, and they are also more compact, and consequently stiffer. These differences offer many possibilities for design, especially when working with high-twist yarns (*see* Chapter 4).

Weave Structures

Although weave structures can be thought of as having certain intrinsic properties, it is important to remember that these are modified by the materials that are used. As Anni Albers makes clear, it is the *interplay* of structure with material that is the essence of weaving. Peter Collingwood nicely captures the way that sometimes the characteristics of the structure will be dominant and sometimes those of the material:

> Although structure is all-important, the physical characteristic of an object is naturally also influenced by the material used in its making. The resulting interaction between material and structure is an absorbing study; for sometimes the material is dominant – compare a silk sari with a wooden fencing panel, both interlaced in plain weave – and sometimes the structure is dominant – compare a felted piano hammer with a knitted Shetland shawl, both made of wool fibre.
>
> Collingwood, 1987

The *sett* (the spacing of the warp *ends* and weft *picks*) also interacts with the weave structure in determining the characteristics of the fabric. For example, plain weave has the maximum number of intersections and so, in principle, can form the firmest structure. In contrast, in twill weaves the yarn passes over and under more than one warp or weft thread, forming a *float*. This structure allows yarns to move more freely, creating more flexible fabrics, with a greater potential for shear in the bias direction and good draping qualities. However, this applies only if all other things are equal. So, for example, a very openly spaced plain weave fabric could break the 'rule' given above and be more flexible than a twill fabric that has been set very closely.

These principles are particularly important when working with high-twist yarns, as it is necessary to allow adequate space for the free movement of these yarns, which will create texture within the fabric. However, this may be achieved either by an open sett or through the structure of the weave (or both). Because a very open plain weave can allow considerable yarn movement, a wide variety of textured effects can be produced in this simple structure, using high-twist yarns and contrasts of material. So it is not essential to be familiar with complex weave structures to design successfully in this way. Chapter 4 is devoted to techniques for working with simple weaves.

However, additional possibilities come into play if the designer is able to exploit weave structures using long floats. Twills are commonly constructed with relatively short floats, with the yarn passing over only a few threads (though longer floats can in principle be used), but many other weave structures are intrinsically characterized by very long floats, so that yarns emerge from the fabric for some distance. These floats allow high-twist yarns complete freedom to spiral, crinkle and contract, and such structures can therefore be used to

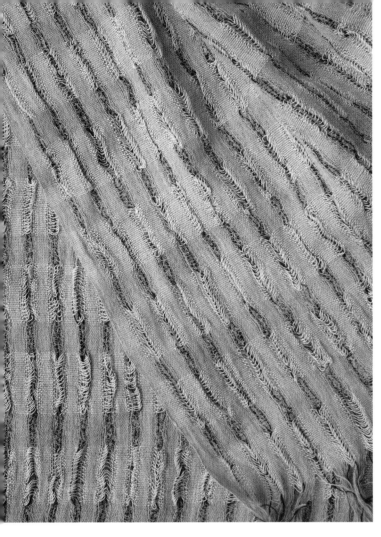

LEFT:
Scarf in linen and silk, with a textured effect in plain weave.

BELOW:
'Square Waves', a double cloth in silk and wool that exploits long floats to create a texture.

produce strongly three-dimensional effects (*see* Chapter 5). More complex weaves, involving two or more layers of cloth, can also be used to create textured effects using high-twist yarns (*see* Chapter 6).

Influence of Yarn Twist on Fabric Properties

Yarn twist has an important influence on the appearance, handle and functional properties of all fabrics, so twist is *always* an important element in textile design. But although the issues covered in this section are relevant to textiles generally, particular emphasis is put on their importance for designs that exploit high-twist yarns.

Uniformity and Openness of Weave

As twist is increased, any yarn unevenness becomes more obvious, as twist accumulates in the thinner areas. Also, as fibres are pressed more closely together, there is a decrease in the diameter of the yarn. This is usually ignored in formulae for calculating yarn diameter – softer spun yarns can be more easily packed together so that an estimate of maximum sett is useful for both hard and soft spun yarns of the same count (*see* Chapter 3 for more about yarn counts, yarn diameter and cloth setting). However, fabrics made with moderately hard-spun yarns do appear more open (voile fabrics exploit this fact) and any unevenness in the yarn is particularly visible in such an open weave. When very highly twisted yarns are used with open setts, the effect is different, because any yarn unevenness becomes less noticeable as yarn movements and the texture of the fabric come to dominate the appearance of the cloth.

Lustre

Lustre is highest when the fibres of a yarn are parallel to the axis of the yarn, so as twist is increased in a singles yarn, lustre will progressively decline. Although silk is the most lustrous of the natural fibres, once the natural gum (sericin) has been removed, crepe silks are singles yarns that are very highly twisted, so they are not lustrous. They often also retain the gum, which further dulls their surface. For plied yarns, the amount of lustre is dependent on the relation between the amounts of twist inserted during the spinning of the singles and that given to the final plied yarn. For the fibres to be parallel to the axis of the yarn, the ratio of the plying twist to the initial spinning twist needs to be 0.7 (assuming that the singles yarns are of the same thickness and that the plying twist is in the opposite direction to the singles twist) and this results in a balanced yarn. Plying is occasionally used for crepe yarns, for example in linen, which is a fairly lustrous fibre, but the plying twist is in the *same* direction as the twist in the singles, to create an unbalanced yarn, so this yarn has a dull surface. Clearly, lustre and a high level of twist cannot be combined within a *yarn*, but lustre can be very effectively used in strongly textured designs, through a suitable combination of high- and low-twist yarns.

Wrinkle Recovery

In general, fabrics woven with yarns of moderate twists give the best balance between wrinkle recovery and maintaining their press after ironing. With very softly twisted yarns, fabrics are so limp that they easily shed creases and also readily lose their press. With hard-spun yarns, fabrics hold their press but also easily retain creases. This is because loosely spun yarns allow fibres to move and escape from pressure, or straighten out when it is removed, while hard-spun yarns restrict fibre movement. However, these principles apply to 'normal', fairly closely set cloths made with yarns that are firmly spun but not highly unbalanced. With very high-twist yarns and open setts, yarn movements come into play and these can produce springy, textured fabrics that resist crushing and creasing.

Shrinkage

Normal shrinkage (as opposed to felting shrinkage) is due to the swelling of textile fibres on wetting, which causes the diameter of the yarn to increase and the fibres to come under stress. The yarn will shrink to relieve this stress, and this effect is most marked with fairly highly twisted yarns, where the fibres are already tightly stretched. Consequently, the amount of shrinkage increases with increased yarn twist. As well as causing shrinkage in many 'normal' fabrics, this swelling reaction is the basis of the textured effects produced in crepe fabrics, because for very high-twist yarns, shrinkage alone is insufficient to relieve the stress and so yarn movements also come into play.

Felting

The felting of wool depends on individual wool fibres responding to heat and agitation by shifting and becoming entangled with one another. This is only possible if the fibres have enough space to move. So, as yarn twist is increased and the yarn becomes more compact, felting is reduced. Direction of twist also has an influence, since when it is the same in warp and weft, a phenomenon called *nesting* comes into play, which restricts the movement of yarn and so reduces felting.

Nesting

When warp and weft are of the same twist, the yarns tend to nest or bed into one another and so produce a firmer but thinner fabric than when opposite twists are used. When a Z pick lies over a Z end the fibres on the underside of the weft pick are in line with those on the upper side of the warp end and this allows the yarns to bed into one another. In contrast, when an S pick lies over a Z end, the fibres lie at 90 degrees to one another – nesting is prevented and the yarns are able to move more freely within the fabric. With yarns of moderate twist, this freedom of movement gives a fuller handle to the fabric.

It might seem implausible that nesting could occur, given that most normal yarns have twist angles between 15 and 30 degrees, and so the fibres could not be expected to line up as shown in the diagram. However, at the point of contact, the fibre angles increase due to the flattening and curling of yarns that naturally takes place in a woven structure.

In the case of very high-twist yarns, it is unclear how much nesting takes place. Since the twist angle may be as high as 40 degrees, the conditions for nesting appear close to perfect – but on the other hand, the extreme compactness of such yarns could *impair* nesting. In practice, a comparison of 'same-twist' and 'opposite-twist' fabrics shows very different patterns of texture (*see* below and Chapter 4). This suggests that nesting is indeed occurring in the case of same-twist interactions. However, yarn movements are also taking place and these are also contributing to the different textures that develop.

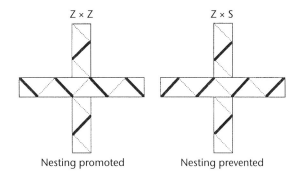

Z × Z   Z × S

Nesting promoted   Nesting prevented

Nesting. The direction of fibre twist is shown as a solid line for the surface of the yarn and as a dotted line for the underside. When the yarns have the same direction of twist (as on the left), the fibres on the underside of the weft yarn will nest with those on the top surface of the warp yarn. When the yarns are of opposite twists, nesting will be prevented.

Yarn Movements and Fabric Texture

Several references have already been made to yarn movements as a response to stress. These movements are the mechanism through which high-twist yarns create fabric texture, so it is helpful to understand exactly how they occur. The basic principles are explained here, but more information is given later (in Chapter 4) about how to exploit these effects in design.

Unbalanced Yarns

The concept of unbalanced yarns has already been briefly introduced, but it is necessary to look at this idea in some detail to make sense of the way that yarn twist influences the texture of fabrics. A singles yarn, especially if it is very highly twisted, is under stress. If a length of such an unbalanced yarn is taken and the two ends brought together, the yarn will ply with itself in the opposite direction to its original twist. During this process, twist is being removed from the individual strands and the stress on these fibres reduced, as they come to lie more in line with the axis of the yarn. If a yarn is allowed to ply naturally in this way, a balanced yarn will be produced – that is, one which shows no tendency to untwist or ply with itself. The amount by which a yarn tends to ply back on itself (the snarling twist) gives a measure of the strain energy or 'liveliness' of the yarn. Singles yarns are necessarily unbalanced. Plied yarns may be balanced, but they are not always so because during manufacture they are not normally allowed to ply naturally (as described above) but have a plying twist applied to them which may be more or less than that required for perfect balance.

Spiralling of Yarns

An alternative way in which an unbalanced yarn can escape from stress is to untwist. If it is restrained at the ends so that this is impossible, it will instead spontaneously curl, attempting to form a spiral in the *same* direction as its twist. It is interesting to contrast this reaction with that of plying (which occurs in the *opposite* direction to the original twist), but a spiral of this type provides another way in which the fibres become more parallel with the length of the yarn, and so relieves the stress on them.

Fabric samples in the loomstate (left) and after wet finishing (right). The different textures of the top and bottom parts of the sample are due to interactions between the warp yarns and wefts of different twist direction. These variations in texture will be discussed in detail in Chapter 4.

Yarns try to spiral in this way even after they are woven, and although restrained by the weave structure, these movements can be sufficient to affect the appearance and handle of the cloth. Some movements may become evident as soon as the fabric is cut from the loom and released from tension, but unbalanced yarns only reveal their full energy when the fabric is wetted out. The fibres absorb water and swell, imposing an additional stress on the yarn, which triggers the reaction, and spiralling movements then occur.

These effects are strongly dependent on the amount of yarn twist, becoming more extreme with increasing twist, but they are also influenced by the sett of the fabric. With closely set cloths, the strain energy of the yarn may only be able to escape at the edges of the cloth, causing the corners of the fabric to flip over. With a more open sett, there is enough space for the energy to be released throughout the fabric, causing a disturbance of the whole surface.

Weave structure also has an impact, because with structures that have fewer intersections, there is more scope for yarn movement. The intrinsic characteristics of the different textile fibres also influence the pattern and extent of this texture. The complex interactions of these various factors form the basis for designing with high-twist yarns, and Chapters 4 to 7 go into detail, showing the various textural effects that are possible.

CHAPTER 2

TWIST AND TEXTURE IN WEAVE DESIGN

Yarn twist has always been an important element in textile design, as it has such a powerful influence on the appearance, handle and functional properties of fabrics. Firmly twisted yarns create very hardwearing fabrics and this will clearly have been a serious, practical issue since the earliest times. However, this book focuses mainly on ways in which yarn twist can become a major element in decorative design and it is reassuring to discover that such techniques also have a surprisingly long history. Some archaeologists represent human prehistory as a time of misery and desperation, and it is easy to imagine the lives of our ancestors as merely a struggle for existence, devoid of pleasure. The record of textiles (admittedly a patchy one, due to random chances of preservation) presents a more encouraging picture. Even in the distant past, people chose to make beautiful as well as functional textiles. Also, the vital factor in textile design has always been the inventiveness of the weaver rather than the complexity of the equipment. So it is not surprising that beautiful fabrics, exploiting high-twist yarns and different directions of twist, have been made on equipment ranging from backstrap looms to computer-controlled Jacquards.

This fabric by the Canadian weaver Mary Frame exploits high-twist yarns of both S and Z twist to create an exuberantly textured effect. (Photo: Carol Sawyer)

Shadow Stripes and Checks

Yarns can be twisted in two different directions, indicated by the letters S and Z (*see* Chapter 1), and these reflect light differently. Stripes of the different twists can be used in warp, weft or both to create 'shadow' stripes and checks, even if all the yarn is the same colour. In the case of strongly warp- or weft-faced plain weave, Z and S stripes can produce an illusion of reversing diagonal lines, giving an effect reminiscent of a herringbone twill. These illusory twill lines appear to run in the opposite direction to that of the yarn twist, so that Z yarn produces an S line, while S yarn produces a Z line (*see* Chapter 4).

Early examples of these techniques have been found in Denmark, where acidic soil conditions have resulted in some exceptionally well preserved textiles. A Bronze Age burial at Borum Eshøj, dated 1400–1200BC, included a beautiful warp-faced belt with stripes of yarn twisted S-Z-S, creating the herringbone effect described above. Wool of a slightly different colour was used for the central stripe, so enhancing the contrast between the different twists.

By the Iron Age (AD100–300), Danish weavers had become extremely accomplished at exploiting shadow techniques of patterning, and complex checks in both plain weave and twill were being produced (*see* Margrethe Hald's book on ancient Danish textiles (1980) for impressive examples). Textiles using similar shadow effects have also been found in the salt mines at Hallstatt, Austria. It seems likely that these techniques were widely known in the ancient world, but because textiles are poorly preserved under most conditions, only a few examples survive.

Yarns with different *amounts* of twist also reflect light differently, even if they are twisted in the same direction, so this provides another way to create shadow effects. Sometimes

The Borum Eshøj burial. The plain weave belt is patterned by a combination of S and Z twist and different coloured yarns. This burial is on display at the National Museum of Denmark, Copenhagen. (Photo: Alan Costall)

This fabric from Southwest China is patterned with shadow stripes. The effect is enhanced with variations in yarn density and thickness, as the stripes of fine Z-twist yarn are set at twice the density of the thicker S-twist yarn. (Designer unknown, Gina Corrigan Collection)

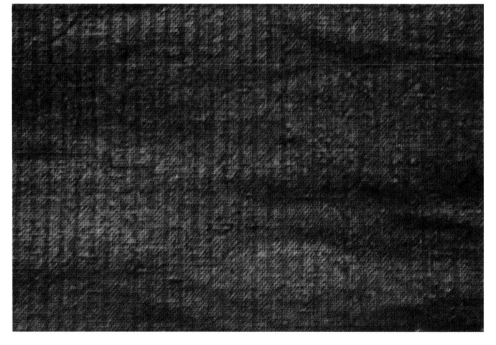

A jacket from Southwest China, showing a shadow check. (Designer unknown, Gina Corrigan Collection)

several factors work together to give the effect: for example, yarns with a high twist are also more compact than lower-twist ones, and so give a more open fabric. Shadow effects can also be further emphasized by other factors, such as yarns of different thickness or variations in the sett. Shadow patterning has continued in use into modern times, particularly in handweaving, for example among minority populations in rural China. It is also used on an industrial scale to give subtle stripe effects in fine suiting.

Textured Textiles

Early Textiles

The use of highly twisted yarns to create textured fabrics goes back at least to ancient China, a fragment of silk from the Shang dynasty (1600–1027 BC) being a very early example. A tomb from the Warring States period (475–221 BC) has remains of a fabric in which yarns of both S and Z twist were used in the warp, with S twist in the weft. The technique of alternating S and Z twists in the warp, weft or both to create an overall crinkled texture (crepe) continues to this day.

It is possible that the ancient Egyptians were aware of the possibilities of yarn twist for creating textured effects, even

though no fabrics have been found where yarn twist is definitely creating such an effect. A dress dated to the fifth dynasty (2498–2345 BC) showed some signs, while being conserved, that it might have been designed to pleat spontaneously. A description of this dress is given by the Egyptologist, Rosalind Janssen (formerly Hall), who also draws attention to wall paintings from the eighteenth dynasty that may represent such natural pleating (Hall, 1986a, b). For example, the beautiful paintings from the tomb of Nebamun (c. 1350 BC), now at the British Museum, show people wearing garments with rippled pleats, very different from the usual representations of pleated garments in most Egyptian wall paintings.

Unlike the Chinese, the ancient Egyptians used only one direction of yarn twist, S, for their woven fabrics. Had high-twist yarns been used, this would have produced an effect of fine, irregular pleating (crepon) rather than an overall crinkled texture (see Chapter 4). Close examination of ancient Egyptian linen fabrics has revealed that relatively high levels of yarn twist were quite commonly used (Kemp and Vogelsang-Eastwood, 2001). I have experimented with modern, commercial linen yarns, including some with 'crepe twist', and others that I have twisted up to levels comparable with ancient Egyptian yarns. I have used these for woven samples with various arrangements of 'cramming and spacing' to simulate the structure of ancient Egyptian linens. My samples confirm that there would have been sufficient twist in many ancient Egyptian linen yarns to cause spontaneous pleating

ABOVE:
This Japanese silk kimono fabric shows the 'classic' crepe texture, produced by alternations of yarn twist (2Z, 2S) in the weft. (Designer unknown)

BELOW:
Samples woven to test the idea of 'natural' pleating in ancient Egypt. A 'crammed and spaced' arrangement has been used to mimic the effect normally found in ancient Egyptian textiles. This occurred because Egyptian looms had no reeds, but only a system for spacing yarns in groups. A sample of the fabric in its loomstate is shown at the bottom of the picture, while an identical fabric, after wet finishing, is shown at the top.

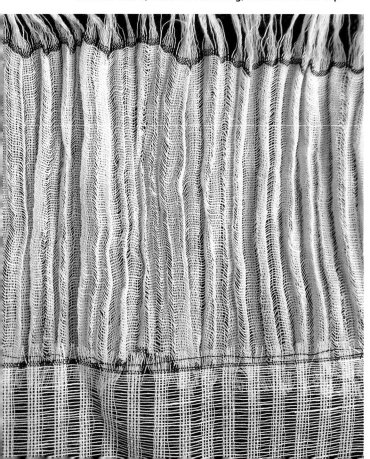

A banquet scene from Nebamun's tomb shows guests wearing clothes with rippled pleats.
(Photo: Alan Costall)

when the fabrics were wetted out, provided that they were very openly woven. Written sources from ancient Egypt indicate that various different fabric qualities were recognized (Hall, 1986b), so it is possible that a naturally pleated texture was known and used.

Both the fine crinkled texture given to fabrics through the crepe technique (mixing Z and S twists) and the crepon texture (using only one direction of twist) have continued to be used, though the popularity of these effects has varied in different periods and cultures. As well as creating an interesting texture, the crinkling or pleating gives elasticity to the fabric and this quality has been much valued for garments, particularly those with a very simple cut. Dorothy Burnham refers to a woman's shirt from Greece (mid-nineteenth century), which has the side section of the garment running up to form part of the sleeve. She comments that the success of this unusual cut is dependent on the elasticity of the material that has been used:

The wearing of shirts made in this way was fairly widespread in Turkey, Greece and the Aegean Islands. . . The material is a heavily creped weave of silk, cotton or a mixture of the two. The actual width of the one shown is 41cm (16in) but it pulls in to about 25cm (10in).

Burnham, 1973, p. 23

In ancient Peru, highly twisted yarns were extensively used for a range of textiles but are most noticeable in the gauze weaves, for which the Peruvians are justly famous. Mary Frame has described her studies of Peruvian gauzes and how she carefully replicated them, using balanced, plied linen yarns. Although she was able to reproduce the structures perfectly, she was disappointed to find that her replications lacked the character of the originals.

> The most beautiful gauzes (Chancay style, central Coast, AD900–1400) are made of overtwisted cotton singles. The energy of the yarn pulls the openings into graceful ovoids and compresses the dense areas into curved outlines. This lively tension, so central to the appeal of the fabrics, was missing in my replications, providing an unforgettable lesson in the importance of fiber choice and twist degree.
>
> Mary Frame, 1986, p. 28

Twentieth Century to Today

The fine texture of the crepe effect, known for thousands of years, has continued to be valued up to the present day, though its popularity has fluctuated as fashions have varied. The French dressmaker Madeleine Vionnet produced beautiful and innovative bias-cut dresses in crepe during the 1920s and 1930s. The drape of fine crepe fabrics was especially suitable for the bias cut, and Vionnet's groundbreaking technique was widely copied during the 1930s. Although crepe subsequently became less popular as fashions changed, it has continued to be used when flexible, fluid effects are required and today is regarded as one of the classic fashion fabrics.

However, towards the end of the twentieth century, new developments took place in the design of textured textiles. Two different groups of people began to experiment with high-twist yarns, with a view to creating effects that were bolder than those of traditional crepe fabrics.

Working on an industrial scale, the Japanese designer Junichi Arai began to use high-twist yarns in the 1970s and 1980s, producing boldly patterned and textured fabrics for fashion designers, such as Issey Miyake. Traditional textiles and techniques have been a great inspiration to Arai, but he has used these ideas to make *new* textiles, working with modern methods. As well as making extensive use of the high-twist yarns that had traditionally been used in Japan, he also developed new yarns and fabrics, working with the many small mills in Kiryu, where he lives. Arai, who has been called

the best 'textile planner' in the world, combines a profound understanding of yarn properties with expertise in the latest technology. He is able to exercise great control in playing off different yarn qualities against one another and often uses weave structure in subtle ways, to create striking effects through essentially simple means. Arai's work has been widely admired; in 1987, the Royal Society of Arts made him an Honorary Royal Designer for Industry, and in 2011 he was awarded an Honorary Doctorate by the Royal College of Art.

In 1984, Arai co-founded the Nuno Corporation, together with another Japanese designer, Reiko Sudo. Nuno (which means 'fabric' in Japanese) rapidly became famous for innovative textile design and a willingness to mix simple hand techniques with state-of-the-art technology in pursuit of an idea. Arai later left Nuno to pursue his own work, and he has continued to experiment widely, both with high-twist yarns and with a variety of unusual materials. Since then, Nuno has been under the leadership of Reiko Sudo, and continues to have an extremely high reputation for imaginative and adventurous design. Nuno's work has been beautifully recorded in a series of books, and their website also provides many illustrations, together with a history of the company.

At about the same time, a new interest in strongly textured textiles was also beginning to develop within the handweaving community. The weaver Anne Blinks drew attention to the disturbances produced by overtwisted yarns, showing her samples of textured fabrics to interested handweavers (Mary Frame recalls that one of these was nicknamed 'the ace bandage' in reference to the traditional use of overtwist for crepe bandages). Anne Blinks also coined the term 'collapse', which has since become widely used among handweavers, especially as a way to refer to relatively large-scale effects, as compared with the very fine-scale texture of traditional crepes. Anne Blinks's observations were followed up by Sharon Alderman, Lillian Elliot and Mary Frame. Their intriguing and informative articles, written in the mid 1980s, have been largely responsible for bringing ideas about high-twist yarns to a wide audience of handspinners and weavers.

However, an initial difficulty for handweavers was that industrial crepe yarns were not easily available, so much of the early work on very highly twisted yarns, for example by Mary Frame, was carried out by handspinning the yarn or adding twist to commercial yarns. Although this allowed great flexibility of design, it made the work very labour intensive and obviously excluded handweavers who were not also spinners. This situation was, in fact, a special case of the general difficulty of obtaining industrial yarns of all kinds in the small

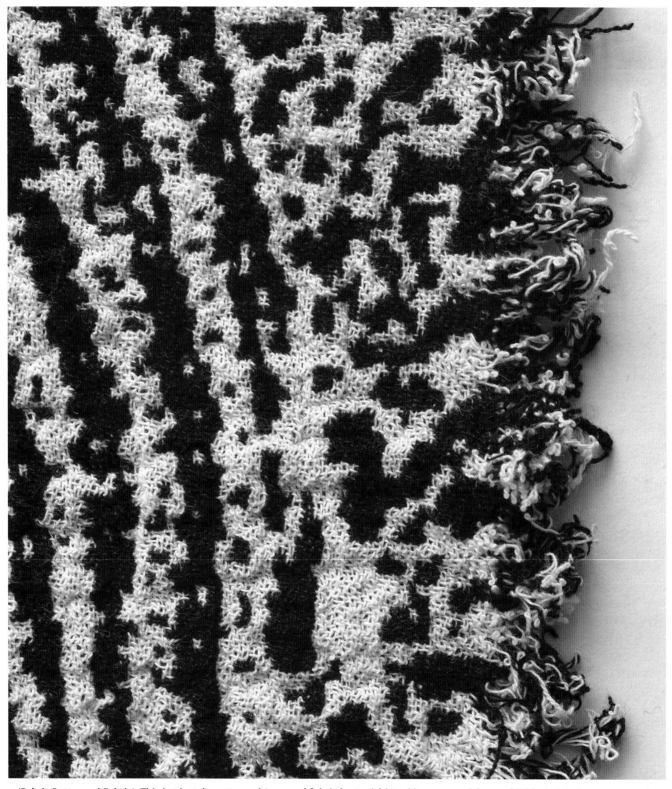

'Fabric Patterned Fabric': This intricately patterned Jacquard fabric by Junichi Arai is woven with very highly twisted cotton yarns in both warp and weft. The fabric shrank in width from 160cm to 90cm during finishing, creating an elastic fabric with a finely crimped surface. (Ann Sutton Collection)

'Film', a double cloth scarf by Reiko Sudo, the co-founder of Nuno. A lightly overtwisted cotton weft yarn creates a gentle crepon effect in both layers of cloth.

These wool samples were woven by Sharon Alderman (USA) while she was investigating the phenomenon of 'tracking' or 'crow's foot', a textured effect that often arises in plain weave fabrics when they are wet finished. She found that the amount of yarn twist and the sett of the cloth were crucial factors in controlling the effect. These samples at different setts show that there is no tracking if the fabric is closely woven (top), very pronounced tracking with an intermediate sett (bottom), and extreme tracking with a very open sett (centre). (Photo: Joe Coca. Originally published in *Handwoven* in 1985. *See* Bibliography for details of the original article. Copyright *Handwoven* magazine.)

quantities normally required by handweavers. In 1998, a group of Danish textile designers decided to tackle this problem and, with the help of a grant from the Danish Design Fund, set up the Yarn Purchasing Association (in Danish *Garnindkøbsforening*, usually shortened to GIF). This association now distributes a wide range of unusual yarns, including a good selection of industrial crepe yarns. One of the founding members, Lotte Dalgaard, who has since become one of the most prominent handweavers in this field, nicely expresses the excitement felt by most people when they first begin to work with high-twist yarns:

> It was a wonderful experience for me when I wet finished the cloth. I never dreamt the overspun yarn would have such a great effect on the whole structure of the textile. The slightly stiff linen and hemp threads lay in the most beautiful waves, because the crepe yarns contracted and became shorter. A delightful new world opened up before me, after forty years as a weaver with everything tight and neat and with geometrical designs. Always nicely pressed and with even edges. All this was completely overturned – it was wonderful to have a fresh starting point with these new yarns and the possibilities they opened up.
>
> Lotte Dalgaard, 2007, p. 15, translation by Ann Richards

Structural Textures

Though most of the early uses of yarn twist involved simple weaves, high-twist yarns also work well when used with other structures, and although this approach does not go back to the very earliest times, many of the techniques used today do have historical precedents. With some weaves, the effect of the structure is powerful enough to produce texture even with 'normal' yarns, but more highly twisted yarns have also sometimes been used with these structures, when a very strongly textured effect was required. The use of weave structures together with high-twist yarns will be discussed in detail in Chapters 5, 6 and 7.

One technique that has attracted particular interest is an effect of soft pleating, produced by using weaves that have warp floats on one face and weft floats on the other. These structures have traditionally been used to create block and stripe arrangements of various kinds, using the two faces of the weave, and have often been intended simply as flat patterning devices.

In other cases there has been a deliberate intention to create a subtle texture. For example, Watson (1954) describes one type of dimity as a cloth intended for bed covers, which

A fabric in linen and crepe wool, with a copper/polyamide selvedge, by the Danish weaver Lotte Dalgaard. (Photo: Ole Akhøj)

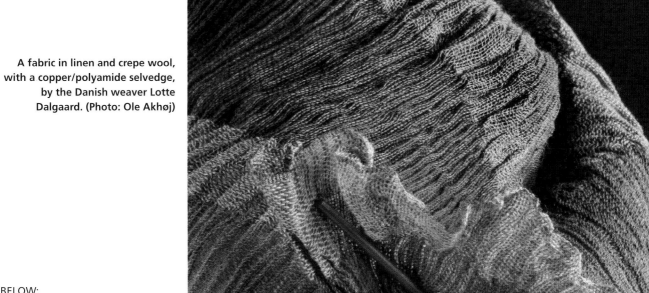

BELOW:
A group of pleated scarves. Warp: spun silk, tussah and silk noil. Weft: tussah silk.

Handwoven cotton tea towel from Blindes Arbejde, made in Denmark by blind weavers. The *drejl* technique has produced contrasting blocks of colour, but without creating a texture. (Designer unknown)

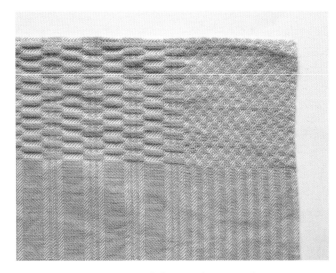

Tea towel from the Swedish firm Växbo Lin, with cotton warp and linen weft. The unbalanced cotton warp causes the *dräll* blocks to develop a textured effect, but only in the warp direction. (Designer unknown)

was woven with very narrow stripes of alternate faces of the weave, to create a ridged effect. Oelsner (1952) describes a related technique that produces a faintly ridged texture, which he calls a 'tricot weave', because of its resemblance to knitting. In fact the ridged or pleated texture is relatively easy to produce unintentionally, and many weavers must have done this while trying to produce other effects. I did so myself, as a beginner at weaving, while trying to weave a smooth, flat scarf. Although the effect was not what I was aiming for at the time, I was struck by its potential and went on to develop and use it extensively for both garments and scarves.

Other weavers have discovered the same effect by observing fabrics where the structure has been used with the intention of creating pattern, but which have also developed a subtle unintended texture. These weave structures are often used for table linens and tea towels, especially in Scandinavia, where this type of patterning is known as *dräll* (Sweden), *drejl* (Denmark) or *dreil* (Norway). For these purposes a textured effect is not generally desired, but it may begin to arise naturally in areas of the fabric where there are relatively long, thin stripes, especially if unbalanced yarns have been used. Examples are given here showing how the technique may produce either a flat pattern or a more textured effect. The Danish tea towel has been woven with balanced yarns, wide stripes and an open sett, and it simply produces coloured blocks without texture. In contrast, the Swedish cloth has an unbalanced cotton warp, with narrow stripes and a close sett, and the fabric has developed a faintly ridged texture at the very edge of the cloth, but only in the warp direction. If the lengthways stripes are examined, it will be seen that these are kept completely flat by the stiffer linen weft. Very frequent reversals of the structure, as seen in the chequerboard effect at the corner of the towel, also tend to subdue the texture. These various effects will be discussed in more detail in Chapters 5 and 10.

These unintended textural effects are usually most noticeable at the very edges of the cloth. The innovative German handweaver, Andreas Möller, noticed precisely this type of texture developing at the edge of a cotton tablecloth he had woven. Intrigued by the effect, he went on to experiment with the same structure, using a variety of different yarns, in an attempt to create a more definite texture. This resulted in his range of boldly pleated designs for scarves and throws. Möller is a designer who carefully attends to things that occur by chance in his fabrics and then uses these in an imaginative way as a source of new ideas. This type of reflective approach to weave design will be discussed in more detail in Chapter 10.

Over the last twenty years, this technique has become increasingly popular and has been used a great deal for scarves. There has also been an interesting twist on its use in table-cloths. Traditionally these were intended to be flat, so any unwanted texture that arose during washing would be ironed out. But recently Växbo Lin has used this type of structure to produce a tablecloth that is *supposed* to develop a texture. When you buy the cloth it is unfinished, and only after the first wash will it develop its 'proper' ridged texture. The customer is warned to expect shrinkage!

A Brief History of Twist

This has been a very brief survey, not because the history itself is brief, since some techniques go back thousands of years, but because there is a limited amount of material available. Also, some particularly useful techniques, such as shadow stripes/checks and crepe, were early brought to such a state of perfection that they have continued in use almost unchanged. However, in spite of this early technical mastery of certain types of cloth, there is still plenty of scope for experimenting with yarn twist, and the rest of this book sets out to demonstrate some of the possibilities for contemporary textile design.

A pleated scarf by Andreas Möller. A wide variety of interesting designs, some boldly textured and others more subtle, can be seen on his website. (Photo: Andreas Möller)

Samples of a textured linen tablecloth 'Våga', produced by the Swedish firm, Växbo Lin. The fabric is shown in the loomstate and after washing (*see* also Chapter 5). (Designer: Ingela Berntsson)

CHAPTER 3

MAKING SENSE OF YARNS

Yarn Counts

The thickness of a yarn is indicated by its *count*, and several different count systems are currently in use. In some cases, the count is based on a fixed weight and the length of yarn equivalent to this weight. These are *indirect* yarn count systems, and increasing yarn numbers indicate finer yarns. Alternatively, the yarn count may be based on a fixed length of yarn, for which the weight is given. These systems are *direct*, and the higher the yarn number, the thicker the yarn. A large number of count systems were developed for different textile fibres and industries, but most of them have now fallen out of use. A few that are still in common use are given here, though these traditional counts, most of which were based on yards/lb, are being rapidly displaced by metric systems. A proposed universal direct system, Tex, was introduced in an attempt to rationalize the situation, but although this has been adopted by some parts of the textile industry, it is far from universal. It seems to have suffered the fate of Esperanto – an excellent idea, but not enough people speak it. A popular alternative is the indirect metric count (Nm), and at present, many yarns are sold under this system.

It is important to know the count of a yarn in order to calculate the weight of yarn required for a particular cloth (*see* box). However, the yarn count is also valuable in other ways, since it may be used to estimate the yarn diameter, which is needed for cloth setting and yarn twist calculations (*see* below).

CALCULATING YARN QUANTITIES

First work out the total number of ends in the warp (epi or epcm × width of warp), and then multiply this number by the warp length to give the total length of yarn required. Divide this by the yardage of the yarn, calculated from its count, to find the weight of yarn that will be required. Similar calculations are then carried out for the weft.

Fixed Weight Yarn Count Systems

Traditional Systems

These systems base the count on the number of unit lengths (skeins, hanks and so on) to a fixed *weight*. The yarn becomes finer with increasing count. There are several systems based on yards/lb.

This double cloth uses very different cloth settings for the two layers, in relation to the maximum that would have been possible for each of the yarns. The silk cloth that forms the face of the cloth is set at 36 epi, which is 64 per cent of the maximum possible sett for this yarn. But the wool cloth, which needs space to be able to shrink and throw the face cloth into relief, is set at 18 epi, which is only 50 per cent of the maximum for this yarn. Taking care to record the percentage setts that have been successful is one way to build on experience.

Yarn Type	Unit	Length/lb
Woollen spun – Galashiels	cut	200yd
Woollen spun – Yorkshire	skein	256yd
Worsted (w.c.)	hank	560yd
Linen (lea or Nel)	lea	300yd
Cotton (c.c. or Ne)	hank	840yd
Spun silk	hank	840yd

For example, take a cotton yarn with a count of eight – the cotton unit is 840yd, therefore:

Cotton 8 = 8 × 840 = 6,720yd/lb

When a yarn is plied the count is written with the ply number first, followed by the count of the singles that make up the ply. The resultant yarn is twice as thick and the yards/lb are therefore halved – for example:

$$\text{Cotton 2/8} = \frac{8 \times 840}{2} = 3,360 \text{ yd/lb}$$

Metric System

The metric count is based on km/kg and is normally indicated by Nm (occasionally m.c.). For plied yarns, in the metric system, the count of the component yarns is given first, followed by the ply number – for example:

$$\text{Spun silk 30/2 Nm} = \frac{30,000}{2} = 15,000\text{m/kg}$$

Fixed Length Yarn Count Systems

Fixed length yarn count systems use a fixed length and a variable weight. The yarn therefore becomes thicker with increasing count.

Tex System

The Tex system has been suggested as a universal system, to replace all other count systems. The Tex count is the weight in grams of 1,000m (g/km); for example:

1,000m of a 15 Tex yarn weigh 15g

When a yarn is plied the resultant count is the sum of the component yarns, and the direction of the ply may also be given – for example:

20/2 S indicates a yarn composed of two threads of 10 Tex, plied together with an S twist.

Denier System

The denier system is a traditional system originally developed for filament silk, though it is sometimes also used for man-made extruded fibres. The denier count is the weight in grams of 9,000m; for example:

9,000m of a 40-denier yarn will weigh 40g

In the case of silk, because the thickness and exact number of filaments may vary slightly along the length of the yarn, the count is sometimes stated as a range: for example 20/22 denier. When fine yarns are thrown together to produce heavier yarns, this may also be indicated in the count. For example, a yarn made by throwing together three yarns of count 20/22 may be shown as 3/20/22 or 3 × 20/22. The overall count in this case would be 60/66. However, some manufacturers do not indicate the components or the range, but simply give the resultant average count, which in this case would be 63 denier.

YARN COUNT CONVERSIONS

Fixed weight counts can be converted to Tex:

$$\text{Tex} = \frac{496000}{\text{Yards/lb}} \qquad \text{Tex} = \frac{1000}{\text{km/kg}}$$

Tex counts can be converted to fixed weight counts:

$$\text{Yards/lb} = \frac{496000}{\text{Tex}} \qquad \text{km/kg} = \frac{1000}{\text{Tex}}$$

Denier can be converted to fixed weight counts:

$$\text{Yards/lb} = \frac{4464600}{\text{denier}} \qquad \text{km/kg} = \frac{9000}{\text{denier}}$$

Denier can be converted to Tex:

$$\text{Tex} = \frac{\text{denier}}{9}$$

Finding the Count of Unknown Yarns

It is very useful to be able to estimate the count of an unknown yarn, since there is a considerable trade in mill ends, some of which are not labelled with a yarn count (and some that are mislabelled). This can be done by winding out a known length of yarn and weighing it. How you tackle this task depends on the equipment you have available. It can be most easily done if you have a skein winder that measures the length of the yarn, and a reasonably accurate balance. But acquiring this kind of equipment is probably not justified unless you also frequently wish to make skeins of known length for dyeing.

With simpler equipment, it is still possible to make a rough estimate using a niddy-noddy or other skein winder, provided you establish the length of the skein that it makes. The length of yarn you need to wind will depend on how accurately you are able to weigh the yarn. Dividing the length of the yarn by its weight in grams will give the metric count. An alternative approach, if you frequently buy unknown yarns, is to acquire a McMorran balance, a simple tool that allows you to make a rough estimate of yarn count from a very small sample.

Yarn Diameters in Weave Design

In addition to its use in calculating yarn quantities, the yarn count has a valuable role in estimating the diameter of the yarn, which is the basis of cloth setting and yarn twist calculations. These aspects of weave design are useful for textiles of all types, but are especially important when working with high-twist yarns and textured fabrics because of the sensitivity of many effects to small variations in sett and in yarn twist.

To work out an appropriate sett for a particular yarn, you will need to determine the number of threads of that yarn that would fill one centimetre (or inch) – that is, to make an estimate of yarn diameter. This is often done informally by wrapping the yarn round a ruler to see how many threads fit into a centimetre or an inch, resulting in an estimate usually expressed as wraps/cm (wpcm) or wraps/inch (wpi). Although this method is very traditional and widely used, it

does have some disadvantages, especially with fine yarns. The number may vary depending on the technique of different individuals, because some people may pull firmly on the yarn, flattening it considerably so that far fewer threads fit in, while others may wind more loosely and push the threads together, so getting a higher estimate. A further difficulty is that this technique is very time consuming when working with fine yarns.

An alternative method is to calculate the yarn diameter from the yarn count. This is extremely quick and simple to do. There are several yarn diameter formulae, but the simplest and most convenient is that devised by Ashenhurst (*see* overleaf). He was working in the late nineteenth century and consequently used the imperial system. From measurements of yarns, he found that the diameters/inch are approximately given by the square root of the yards/lb (for an explanation of square roots, *see* box below). However, he found that he could get a more accurate result by slightly reducing this figure, and he also realized that, since yarns of different fibres and spinning methods vary in their bulkiness, it was helpful to vary this reduction for different types of yarn. Note that yarn diameters (like wraps/cm or wraps/inch) are not expressed as fractions, but as whole numbers (for example, a yarn is not described as having a diameter of ½₀in, but rather as having 20 diameters/inch). This is because it is more convenient for calculations of cloth setting and so on to work with whole numbers.

SQUARE ROOTS

▦ If a number is multiplied by itself, the resulting figure is the 'square' of that number – for example: $5 \times 5 = 25$, so 25 is the square of 5.

▦ Finding the square root means reversing this process, where 5 is the square root of 25.

▦ A calculator is necessary for more difficult numbers. Fortunately, even very basic calculators have a key (marked $\sqrt{}$) for calculating the square root.

The Ashenhurst Formula for Yarn Diameters

Yarn diameters per inch = $\sqrt{\text{yards/lb}}$

Multiply by:
 0.85 for woollen yarns
 0.90 for worsted yarns
 0.92 for cotton, silk and linen

For example: find the diameters per inch of a linen yarn 12 lea.

The unit of linen yarns (lea) = 300yd, therefore linen 12 has 12 × 300 = 3,600yd/lb.

Diameters/ inch
 $= 0.92 \sqrt{\text{yards/lb}}$
 $= 0.92 \sqrt{3600}$
 $= 0.92 \times 60$
 $= 55$

Fifty-five threads of this yarn will fill one inch.

Results from the Ashenhurst formula can easily be converted to the metric system. To convert diameters/inch to diameters/cm, divide by 2.54. Alternatively, a metric version can be used to work directly from m/kg.

The Metric Version of the Ashenhurst Formula

Yarn diameters per cm = $\sqrt{\text{m/kg}}$

Multiply by:
 0.236 for woollen yarns
 0.25 for worsted yarns
 0.255 for cotton, silk and linen

For example, find the diameters/cm of a spun silk yarn 30/2 Nm.

Spun silk 30/2 Nm = $\dfrac{30,000}{2}$ = 15,000 m/kg

Diameters/cm
 $= 0.255 \sqrt{\text{m/kg}}$
 $= 0.255 \sqrt{15,000}$
 $= 0.255 \times 122.5$
 $= 31.2$

Thirty-one threads of this yarn will fill one centimetre.

Comparison of Yarn Diameter Estimates by Ashenhurst and by 'Wrapping'

It is important to realize that the estimates of yarn diameter made by calculation and by wrapping are not the same. No matter how carefully the wrapping technique is carried out, the yarn does tend to become flattened to some extent, and so fewer threads occupy a centimetre (or inch) than theory would predict. The estimate also varies for different individuals, especially with very fine yarns. When I carried out a comparison with a group of students, the estimates obtained by wrapping varied between 60–80 per cent of the figure given by Ashenhurst's formula. On average, a wrapped estimate is likely to give only approximately two-thirds of the figure given by the formula. You need to keep this in mind when making calculations that depend on yarn diameter, such as those for cloth setting and yarn twist.

Clearly there are advantages in sticking to one system or the other, but if you choose to mix them, it may be worth doing some work to compare your wrapped estimates with Ashenhurst. Wrapped estimates carried out carefully by one person may bear a fairly consistent relationship to Ashenhurst, and if you know what percentage this is, then it may be possible to use both systems – for example, wrapping for coarse yarns and Ashenhurst for fine ones.

Knowing your personal results for a wrapped estimate, as compared with Ashenhurst, will also allow you to make use of information in this book about cloth settings for different types of fabric, expressed as percentages of maximum sett (see below), since these relate to yarn diameters derived by the Ashenhurst formula.

Cloth Setting

Basic Principles of Cloth Setting

The number of yarn diameters that fill one centimetre (or inch) can be used, together with a cloth-setting formula (given below), to make an estimate of a suitable sett for a fabric made from that yarn. It is important to realize that, though helpful, this is not a substitute for relying upon personal judgement. The formula is a very useful starting point for sampling, but it cannot determine the *correct* sett for any particular cloth

– many other factors must be taken into account, and making these judgements is the designer's job!

The cloth-setting formula is very simple and makes the assumption that you are weaving a balanced cloth, using a yarn of the same thickness for both warp and weft; however, on many occasions this will not be true. Of course, more complex calculations could be made to take account of variations, such as the weft being finer or thicker than the warp, or a requirement for the cloth to be warp- or weft-faced. However, given that the calculated cloth setting is merely a starting point for sampling, in practice it is very convenient to use the sett, as calculated by this simple formula, as a fixed reference point.

If diameters/cm (or diameters/inch) have been calculated by the Ashenhurst method, the cloth-setting formula will give a very close sett, best regarded as a maximum. This will make a very firm cloth – too firm for many purposes. Even furnishing fabrics might be set lower, for example at 90–95 per cent of this figure. Clothing fabrics could be set at 60–80 per cent, depending on their use, and lightweight scarves and shawls even lower. If high-twist yarns are being used, setts of 50 per cent or even less are often necessary to allow enough space for the yarn to shrink and spiral.

If diameters/cm (or diameters/inch) have been estimated by wrapping, rather than calculation, the cloth-setting formula will probably give a figure somewhere between 60 per cent and 80 per cent of that given by the Ashenhurst method. Wrapping therefore gives a figure that is best regarded as a good sett for a medium-weight or 'average' fabric, rather than a maximum sett. So if you are starting from a wrapped estimate, any information given in this book about percentage settings needs to be adjusted. Assuming that a wrapped estimate is, on average, two-thirds that of Ashenhurst, any estimate derived by wrapping needs to be increased by half to give the same figure. For example a lightweight scarf set at 50 per cent of the maximum (Ashenhurst) would need to be set at 75 per cent of a wrapped estimate. If, by experiment, you find that your personal wrapped estimates are higher or lower than this, then you can make adjustments accordingly.

Cloth-Setting Formula

In working out the sett, allowance is made for the space taken up by the weft, as it intersects with the warp. For example, in a balanced plain weave, only *half* of the threads that would fill a centimetre (or inch) can be used for the warp, as the rest of the space is needed for the weft.

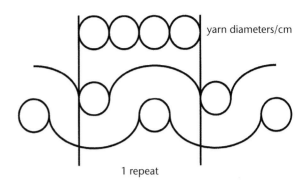

yarn diameters/cm

1 repeat

Cloth setting for a plain weave fabric.

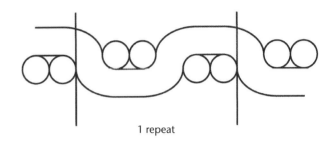

1 repeat

Cloth setting for a twill fabric.

The method of working out the sett, for any weave, is to divide the *number of warp ends* in a repeat of the weave (for plain weave this is two) by the *number of warp ends + number of weft intersections* (for plain weave there are two warp ends and two intersections, so 2 + 2 = 4).

For plain weave:

$$\frac{2}{4} = \frac{1}{2} \qquad \text{Sett} = \frac{1}{2} \times \text{yarn diameters/cm}$$
$$\text{(or yarn diameters/inch)}$$

In a 2/2 twill there are four warp ends in a repeat and two intersections.

For 2/2 twill:

$$\frac{4}{4+2} = \frac{4}{6} = \frac{2}{3} \qquad \text{Sett} = \frac{2}{3} \times \text{yarn diameters/cm}$$
$$\text{(or yarn diameters/inch)}$$

General Formula

The sett for any weave can be worked out in the following way:

$$\text{Sett} = \left(\frac{\text{No. of warp ends in a repeat}}{\text{No. of warp ends +}\ \text{No. intersections in a repeat}} \right) \times \begin{array}{c}\text{yarn diameters/cm}\\ \text{(or inch)}\end{array}$$

This general formula is not, however, ideal for weaves with a large number of very long floats. These loose weaves may need to be set rather closer than the formula suggests. Watson (1954, pp. 126–130, *see* Bibliography) gives suggestions for various fabrics, taking account of the different weave structures. For example, in the case of honeycomb (waffle) weaves, his advice is first, to calculate the diameters/inch for the yarn, then the sett for plain weave, and finally to take an average of the two as a suitable setting. For cord weaves with a plain weave face, a similar compromise between the diameters/inch and a plain weave setting is suggested, on the grounds that only half the picks are interlacing with the face. After three pages of such rules of thumb, he finally remarks: 'No hard and fast rules are laid down, as the correct setting of cloths is very largely a matter of good judgment, but theory can be made a very useful adjunct to practice.' As Watson's classic book was first published in 1912, this comment is 100 years old – but it remains excellent advice!

Cloth Setting Using Metric and Imperial Measures

Some of the fabric examples in this book give cloth settings in imperial measures, while others use the metric system. Although this may seem confusing, it is necessary to accept that these systems will continue to run side by side within woven textiles for some time. In much of the world, the metric system is now used exclusively, but in England and the USA, imperial measures are still widely used. This situation is unlikely to change quickly, partly because reeds are so expensive that few weavers could afford to discard imperial reeds that they have used for many years in order to 'go metric'. Also, samples that have been woven using imperial reeds continue to provide a valuable record of experience on which to base new work, even if this is to be carried out using metric reeds. It is best to become familiar with the conversion factors necessary to move easily between the two systems.

CONVERSION FACTORS

To convert:	Multiply by:
yards to metres	0.9144
metres to yards	1.0936
epi to epcm	0.3937
epcm to epi	2.54
ounces to grams	28.35
grams to ounces	0.035
pounds to kilos	0.454
kilos to pounds	2.205
metres/kg to yards/lb	0.496
yards/lb to metres/kg	2.016

REED AND SETT CONVERSION TABLE (CM TO INCHES)

Reed Conversions

Dents/10cm	Dents/in	2 Ends/Dent	3 Ends/Dent
30	7.62	15.24	22.86
35	8.89	17.78	26.67
40	10.16	20.32	30.48
45	11.43	22.86	34.29
50	12.70	25.40	38.10
55	13.97	27.94	41.91
60	15.24	30.48	45.72
65	16.51	33.02	49.53
70	17.78	35.56	53.34
75	19.05	38.10	57.15
80	20.32	40.64	60.96
85	21.59	43.18	64.77
90	22.86	45.72	68.58
95	24.13	48.26	72.39
100	25.40	20.80	76.20
110	27.94	55.88	83.82
115	29.21	58.42	87.63
120	30.48	60.96	91.44

The question of reed sizes is particularly important because these cannot be exact conversions. Although the obvious approach is to take the nearest comparable reed size, any samples from which you are working should also be considered. For example, if working from an existing sample that seems rather firmly woven, it may be better to go to the

REED AND SETT CONVERSION TABLE (INCHES TO CM)

Dents/inch	Dents/cm	2 Ends/dent	3 Ends/dent
8	3.15	6.30	9.45
10	3.94	7.88	11.82
12	4.72	9.45	14.16
14	5.51	11.02	16.53
16	6.30	12.60	18.90
18	7.09	14.17	21.27
20	7.87	15.74	23.61
22	8.66	17.32	25.98
24	9.45	18.90	28.35
28	11.02	22.05	33.06
30	11.81	23.62	35.43

nearest reed size *below*, in the other system, even if it is not the closest. The boxes give conversion charts for the more commonly used reed sizes. For other reed sizes, use the conversion factors.

Using Yarn Diameters and Percentage Sett as Design Tools

Keeping records of the combinations of yarn diameters used in particular designs can be a very useful way of building upon experience. Through sampling, certain relationships between yarns of different thickness may be found to work very well, and these *relationships* (rather than the actual thicknesses of the yarns as such) can be used to guide future work, using different yarns. For example, some structures work particularly well when the warp yarn is about twice the diameter of the weft yarn. Transposing this relationship to new combinations of yarns can be a helpful guide when starting to sample.

In a similar way, I have found it is useful to relate the calculated maximum sett to the percentage of the figure that is finally chosen for the actual piece of work. If, after sampling, the best sett for a scarf proves to be 55 per cent of the maximum sett for that yarn, then this is useful information that can provide a starting point for future work. If you wish to make a similar scarf but in a thicker or finer yarn, first work out the diameter of the new yarn and its maximum sett, and then take 55 per cent of this, and use it as a starting point for sampling for the new scarf. This sett will not necessarily be perfect,

since yarns vary in other ways than merely their diameters, and many other issues may also be relevant to the choice of sett, but it is likely to provide a better starting point than simply guessing. Similar calculations can be made for the setting of the weft. More information about this way of building on experience will be given in Chapters 5 and 10. Of course, the same approach can be used when working from a 'wrapped' estimate of yarn diameter, but such estimates are not as consistent as those derived by the Ashenhurst formula.

COVER

In this book, the cloth-setting formula (which takes account of the structure – plain weave, twill and so on) is used to derive a maximum sett. The actual sett used for a cloth can then be recorded as a percentage of this figure. However, in industry, an alternative concept of *cover* is used to indicate how closely a cloth is set. The *fractional cover* records the fraction of the available space in a cloth that is occupied by yarn. It is found by dividing the ends/cm (or inch) by the yarn diameters/cm (or inch). For example:

A yarn with 120 diameters/inch is set at 60 epi
Fractional cover = 60/120 = 0.5 (or 50 per cent)

Clearly, in the case of plain weave, the fractional cover will be *half* the figure calculated as the percentage sett, because no allowance has been made for the space occupied by the weft (that is, the sett of 60 epi given in the example as 50 per cent cover would be the maximum sett – 100 per cent – for that yarn). So for plain weave, the fractional cover is really providing the same information about cloth density as the sett, and because it is simpler to calculate, you may prefer to use it for your records rather than working with the cloth-setting formula.

However, moving beyond plain weave, fractional cover takes no account of weave structure, so you must expect that the cover for other weaves, such as twills, will be higher than for a plain weave fabric at an equivalent percentage sett. Provided that this is taken into account (that is, you transpose such cover factors only to new designs using the same structure), recording the fractional or percentage cover can be used to guide future work in just the same way as using the percentage sett.

Angle of Twist

Another aspect of design where yarn diameters prove useful is in understanding yarn twist and the different ways in which it is specified. The amount of twist in a yarn is usually given as turns per inch (tpi) or turns per metre (tpm). Tpm is becoming the usual convention in industry, but handspinners using the metric system will probably find it more practical to use turns per centimetre (tpcm). This way of describing yarn twist is useful in relation to the process of spinning, since delivering a measured draw to a set rate of treadling makes it possible to give a known amount of twist to a yarn. But fine yarns *need* more twist than thicker ones to have the same properties, so tpi or tpcm is of no use in comparing yarns of different count. A more fundamental measure is the angle of twist – the angle that the fibres make with the axis of the yarn. When yarns have the same angle of twist, they will have similar properties in terms of strength, liveliness and so on (assuming that they are spun from the same type of fibre).

When controlling twist during spinning, an alternative to inserting a particular number of tpi (tpcm) is to aim to achieve a specified angle of twist. Also, if you wish to reproduce the properties of a particular yarn while scaling up or down to a finer or coarser count, this can be achieved by spinning to the same angle of twist.

Understanding the *relationship* between tpi (tpcm) and twist angle gives even greater control in spinning. Different angles of twist produce yarn suitable for different purposes. Having chosen a suitable angle of twist, one can calculate the number of tpi (tpcm) required to produce that angle in a range of yarns of different thickness.

Twist Angle	Suitable Use
15° = soft twist	Weft
20° = medium soft twist	Weft
25° = medium twist	Woollen spun warp, textured effects with worsted spun yarns
30° = medium hard twist	Worsted warps, strong texture with worsted spun yarns
35° = hard twist	Texture with woollen yarns, crepes/crepons with worsteds
40–45° = very hard twist	Very strong texture, crepes/crepons with silk

Knowing how tpi (tpm) and twist angle relate to one another can also be useful to weavers working with commercial yarns. Even if you have a yarn where tpi (tpm) is not known, it is still possible to make a rough estimate from the twist angle and the yarn diameter. On the other hand, if the supplier has quoted tpi (tpm), it is possible to work in the reverse direction and calculate the twist angle from the tpi (tpm) and yarn diameter. Since twist angle is a more fundamental measure of twist than tpi (tpm), this is a useful way to assess the twist of commercial yarns and make comparisons between yarns.

Types of High-twist Yarn

Commercial high-twist yarns are spun primarily for the production of crepe fabrics which have a fine, overall crinkled texture, produced by mixing Z and S twist yarns. Wool, silk and rayon are the main fibres used for crepe fabrics. Crepe silks often still retain the sericin or natural gum (silk in the gum is known as raw or hard silk), which gives them a crisper handle than high-twist yarns in other fibres, though this gum can be removed in the finishing process if a softer texture is

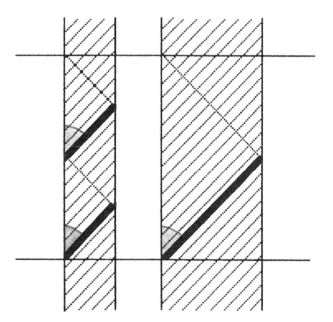

One of these yarns is half the diameter of the other and has twice as many tpi (tpcm), but they both have the same *angle of twist*. Since their degree of twist is the same, they will have similar properties, in terms of strength, liveliness and so on (assuming that they are spun from the same type of fibre).

required. Crepon fabrics, which have a slightly bolder 'tree-bark' texture, are also made from these yarns, but using only one direction of twist. Crepons made from cotton are also common. Linen has not traditionally been regarded as a good creping fibre by the industry, probably due to its lack of elasticity, but some high-twist linen yarns have been produced in recent years, notably by the Italian firm Solbiati, and these will also produce crepon effects.

All these yarns are manufactured for industry, rather than being aimed at handweavers, so they can sometimes be difficult to obtain. Recently, however, because handweavers and designers have made particular efforts to obtain industrial yarns, some of these crepe yarns have become available through a yarn collective in Denmark, the Yarn Purchasing Association (GIF) and some of the more adventurous handweaving suppliers (for example Handweavers Studio in the UK, and Habu in the USA). If yarns are intended for weaving crepe fabrics, the manufacturer will usually specify the turns/inch or turns/metre, and this makes it possible to calculate how highly twisted the yarn is, in terms of its twist angle.

Industrial Twist Factors

In industry it is customary to derive a *twist factor*, for use in calculations, rather than to use the angle of twist directly. This is because information about the yarn count can be incorporated into the twist factor, making it very convenient for someone working with industrial machinery to make rapid calculations for adjustments. However, because there are a number of yarn count systems in operation, there are also different scales of twist factors for these different industries.

I think that it is easier for handspinners and weavers to use *twist angle*, because this is a fundamental geometrical property and is also easy to visualize (with a large angle the yarn *looks* more tightly twisted). It is also useful in communicating with other textile specialists, not connected with the textile industry (archaeologists, historians, and so on), who generally describe yarn twist in this way.

If you are dealing with a small mill, perhaps to get yarn spun to your own specifications, the staff may well describe the amount of yarn twist in terms of the twist factors for their system of spinning. However, they will also know the count of the yarn they are producing and the turns/inch (or turns/metre) they are using. If you ask for these details, you will be able to work out twist angles.

Calculation of Twist Angle and Tpi/Tpcm

The following examples use tpi. However, as the formulae depend on the relationship between yarn diameters and turns/unit length, you can equally well use the metric system, substituting diameters/cm for diameters/in and tpcm for tpi. If you wish to compare handspun yarn with commercial yarn, remember that industry normally works with turns/metre rather than turns/centimetre.

1. FINDING THE TPI FROM THE TWIST ANGLE AND YARN DIAMETER

To find the number of tpi needed to achieve a particular twist angle for a certain thickness of yarn, look up the *tangent of the angle* (*see* table in box overleaf) and use the following formula, rounding off to the nearest whole number.

$$\text{tpi} = \frac{\text{tangent of the twist angle x diameters per inch}}{\pi}$$

$$(\pi = 3.1416)$$

e.g. How many tpi are needed to spin a yarn of thickness 50 diameters/inch and twist angle 30°?

The table gives the tangent of 30° as 0.577

$$\text{tpi} = \frac{0.5774 \times 50}{3.1416} = \frac{28.85}{3.1416} = 9.18$$

A yarn of 50 diameters/inch will need approximately 9 tpi in order to have a twist angle of 30°.

2. FINDING THE TWIST ANGLE FROM THE TPI AND YARN DIAMETER

Although tpi is not usually quoted on 'normal' twist yarns, some suppliers may give details if asked. High-twist (crepe) yarns usually carry this information. Use the following formula:

$$\text{Tangent of the twist angle} = \frac{\pi \times \text{tpi}}{\text{diameters per inch}}$$

When the tangent has been calculated, look it up in the tables to find the closest corresponding angle.

e.g. One supplier offers a yarn with 18 tpi and 72 diameters/inch. Another has a yarn with 24 tpi, but with 104 diameters/inch. Which of them is the most highly twisted?

Yarn A:

$$\text{tan of twist angle} = \frac{3.1416 \times 18}{72} = \frac{56.55}{72} = 0.785$$

In the table this value comes closest to an angle of 38°.

Yarn B:

tan of twist angle = $\dfrac{3.1416 \times 24}{104} = \dfrac{75.4}{104} = 0.725$

The angle given by the table is 36°. Yarn A has a slightly higher twist than yarn B. Both have a high level of twist that is likely to give good crepe effects.

ANGLE-TANGENT TABLE

10°	0.176	22°	0.404	34°	0.675
11°	0.194	23°	0.425	35°	0.700
12°	0.213	24°	0.445	36°	0.727
13°	0.231	25°	0.466	37°	0.754
14°	0.249	26°	0.488	38°	0.781
15°	0.268	27°	0.510	39°	0.810
16°	0.287	28°	0.532	40°	0.839
17°	0.306	29°	0.554	41°	0.869
18°	0.325	30°	0.577	42°	0.900
19°	0.344	31°	0.601	43°	0.933
20°	0.364	32°	0.625	44°	0.966
21°	0.384	33°	0.649	45°	1.000

Using a 'Wrapped' Estimate for Diameters/cm (Diameters/inch)

The yarn twist formulae given here are based on yarn diameters calculated from the yarn count (Ashenhurst formula). If you are estimating the yarn diameters by wrapping, you will obtain an estimate with fewer diameters/cm or inch (due to the flattening of the yarn as it is wrapped). Wrapping will usually give an estimate of about two thirds the diameters/cm (or diameters/inch) given by the Ashenhurst method, so it will be necessary to substitute 2 for π in the yarn twist formulae that are given here. Mabel Ross (1983) gives good, detailed instructions for estimating diameters/inch by wrapping and using this in relation to twist control in handspinning.

Testing Unknown Yarns

As well as using the manufacturer's specifications in the twist angle formulae, it is possible to make measurements of un-known yarns and this information can then be used for calculations in the same way. For example, you can measure the twist angle using a protractor (a magnifying glass or linen tester will be needed for fine yarns). You will find it is not possible to make a precise judgment of the angle, but even a rough estimate can give you useful information. Twist angles vary, even in machine-spun yarn, so measure in several places and take an average.

Alternatively, you can measure the tpcm (tpi) by unwinding a sample of the yarn. Carefully clamp a short length (2cm or 1in) between two clips (small bulldog clips work quite well). Then untwist the yarn by turning one of the clips, counting the number of *complete* turns that are necessary to untwist it. If the yarn resists untwisting, then damp the sample slightly to release tension in the fibres. When you can pass a needle through the fibres from one end of the yarn sample to the other, you can be sure that you have removed all the twist. For fine yarns, you will probably need a magnifier to see this clearly. Yarns vary along their length, so test several samples and take an average.

Adding Twist to Existing Yarns

By taking measurements in this way, you can determine the amount of twist in yarns you already have, even if these are normal yarns where the manufacturer has provided no tpcm (tpi) information. You are then in a position to add twist, to reach a known final twist angle. Although twisting up yarn is fairly time consuming, it is considerably quicker and easier than spinning because you do not have to control the fibres, merely insert twist. It can be very worthwhile in that it greatly extends the range of possibilities, since any of your favourite yarns can be available to you in higher-twist versions. Knowing how your yarns relate to commercial crepes, in terms of their twist, and being able also to consistently produce yarns of a particular degree of twist, gives a great deal of control in designing.

Spinning and Twisting Up Yarns

To insert a known amount of twist, whether you are spinning a yarn or adding extra twist to an existing yarn, you need to know the *twist ratio* of your wheel (that is, the number of turns the flyer makes for each turn of the driving wheel).

In this seersucker fabric, plain weave silk is combined with narrow weft stripes of very highly twisted wool, using a waffle weave (*see* Chapter 5). Although the wool yarn was already highly twisted, further twist was added using a spinning wheel, to create an exceptionally energetic yarn, so that the seersucker effect could be produced with only very narrow stripes of wool. The idea for this fabric came from the 'elastic seersucker' structure of bats' wings.

Put a marker on the flyer, turn the driving wheel by hand through one revolution, and count the number of turns the flyer makes. You can then calculate the number of inches of yarn that must be fed into the wheel per treadle, to achieve any particular tpi.

$$\text{Number of inches per treadle} = \frac{\text{Twist ratio of wheel}}{\text{Required twists per inch}}$$

When adding twist to an existing yarn, a simple rule of thumb is that if you draw off the same length of yarn in inches as the ratio of your wheel, then the number of treadles required to insert enough twist will be the same as the number of tpi you require.

For example, if your ratio is 10 and you draw off 10in of yarn, you will need to treadle five times to insert 5 tpi, eight times to insert 8 tpi, and so on.

It is simple to scale this up or down to accommodate the amount of yarn that you find convenient to handle: for example, with the same wheel you could draw off 20in and treadle ten times, or 30in and treadle fifteen times to obtain 5 tpi.

The same relationship holds if metric measurements are used.

Adding Twist to Linen Yarns

Although linen is strong, it does not respond well to the high levels of stress created by adding large amounts of twist, and fine linens, in particular, may easily break. So I propose that we take a tip from the ancient Egyptians, who passed their linen yarns through water, using special spinning bowls fitted with loops, before adding twist to them. Ancient Egyptian linen was assembled by splicing, as a preliminary stage, before twist was added using a spindle (for more information about yarn construction in ancient Egypt, refer to the very detailed account by Kemp and Vogelsang-Eastwood, 2001, *see* Bibliography). Linen is stronger wet than dry and the fibres also become softened and loosened by the moisture, which allows them to accept the extra twist more easily. The Egyptian method can easily be adapted for the present day – simply place a cup (or other similar object that provides a loop) in a bowl of water, and then run the linen yarn through the cup handle on its way to the spinning wheel. As yarn is drawn off, it passes rapidly through the water and this brief immer-

sion is sufficient to strengthen it. If you intend to use a very fine yarn as warp, you could substitute weak size for water in your 'spinning bowl' so that the yarn will be further strengthened, by being coated with size, at the same time as it is being twisted up. I use a weak solution of Manutex (manufactured as a print paste) as a size, but starch or wallpaper paste (free of pesticides) could also be used.

I have used this technique successfully when twisting up linen yarn, as part of an experiment to investigate the possibility of 'natural' pleating in ancient Egyptian linens (*see* Chapter 2). I untwisted several samples of machine-spun linen yarn and used the twist formulae to determine the angle of twist, which I found to be 16°. Many ancient Egyptian linen fabrics are woven from yarns with much higher levels of twist. Angles of 25–30° are common, and even higher values have been recorded. I calculated the tpi necessary to increase the twist angle of modern machine-spun linen to give various twist angles, in the range 20–36°, and added extra twist to the yarn. I found it essential to use the 'spinning bowl' technique so that the linen yarn would accept these high levels of twist.

Using Yarn and Sett Information

Throughout this book, I have given yarn and sett details for a variety of samples. These are imperial or metric, depending on the reeds that have been used, and the conversion factors given earlier in this chapter can be used, if necessary, to convert them to the alternative system. However, these settings are not intended as rigid recommendations, because higher or lower setts would also have produced satisfactory fabrics in many cases, though with a different drape and texture. But they can be used as general guidance by anyone new to working with high-twist yarns, since the suggested setts do allow sufficient space for these lively yarns to move and create texture. This information can also be used as a guide to the use of other finer or heavier yarns, by using the Ashenhurst formula to calculate the diameters/inch (or cm) and working out the percentage sett (or cover) that has been used. This information can be transposed to other yarns to guide future work. Detailed examples of this way of working will be given in Chapter 10.

Running a linen yarn through water, before adding twist, helps to avoid breakages. The yarn is drawn off the top of the cone, through a hook or over a rod, and then down through the 'spinning bowl'.

Sample woven to test ideas about the possibility of 'natural' pleating in ancient Egypt.
Warp: Linen 77 lea. Weft: *Bottom*: Linen 88 lea. *Centre*: Same yarn with 10° extra twist. *Top*: Same yarn with 15° extra twist. The pleating becomes stronger with increasing twist.
Warp sett: Crammed and spaced setting of three ends/dent for three dents, three empty dents, in a 100/10cm reed (average sett: 15 epcm). Weft sett: 11 ppcm.

45

CHAPTER 4

SIMPLE COMPLEXITY

There are two sorts of truth: trivialities, where the opposite is obviously impossible, and deep truths, which are characterized by their opposite also being a deep truth.

Niels Bohr

Some basic properties of fibres, yarns and weave constructions have already been covered in Chapter 1. The weaving of textiles, especially strongly textured ones, can best be thought of as an emergent process, in which these fundamental elements interact to create entirely new properties in finished fabrics. Often a subtle interplay of many factors is responsible for a particular result, and so, in trying to form theories about what is happening and why, it is common to encounter not only trivial but also deep and apparently contradictory truths. While writing this chapter I have frequently found that I have hardly stated a principle before feeling I must go on to point out that exactly the opposite may also be true!

Textures in Simple Weaves

For anyone who is more interested in materials than in complex weave structures, simple weaves offer immense opportunities for design. High-twist yarns readily create a wide range of textured surfaces, depending on the amount and direction of yarn twist, the fibre and the sett. Further possibilities are offered by the juxtaposition of strongly contrasting materials. Because of the 'emergent complexity' of the interaction of such simple elements, it is not necessary to be deliberately elaborate in order to get richly complex results.

It is also worth paying close attention to what happens in the simplest structures, because so many of these fundamental principles are applicable to other weaves. For example, the techniques of using different yarn twists and setts, or contrasts of material, to create varied textures in plain weave, can also be very effectively applied to more complex structures, such as float weaves and double or multiple layer cloths. This chapter deals mainly with plain weave but a few examples of twill fabrics are included, where the twill has been used to allow freer yarn movement or as a way to pattern the fabric. The use of twills as a structural means to create texture will be covered in Chapter 5.

A scarf by Noriko Matsumoto (Japan). High-twist woollen merino (brown) and ramie (white) yarns are used in the warp. The difference in shrinkage between these yarns creates the textured surface of the fabric. The weft is filament silk. (Photo: Noriko Matsumoto)

Same-Twist and Opposite-Twist Yarn Interactions – Tracking and Undulations

Take the apparently simple situation of a plain weave fabric, with unbalanced yarns in both warp and weft, and a reasonably open sett that allows yarn movement to take place freely. When the direction of twist is the same for both warp and weft (Z × Z or S × S), a characteristic 'tracking' or 'crow's foot' pattern is produced. Within the limits of the weave construction, the yarns are trying to spiral in the same direction as their twist. As successive threads in warp and weft curl in this way, a series of faint diagonal lines form in the fabric, running in both warp and weft directions. The fabric may give

The textural patterns produced by same-twist and opposite-twist yarn interactions. Crepe wool 58/2 Nm, 32 epi, ppi.

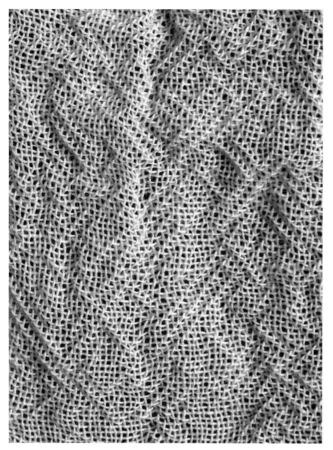

Warp and weft are both Z-twist yarns, giving tracking.

The warp is Z twist and the weft is S twist, and these opposite twists create an undulating texture.

the superficial impression that it has been woven in a diamond twill. Because nesting occurs when yarns of the same twist cross one another (*see* Chapter 1), yarn movement is not completely free, and so this textural pattern is rather small in scale.

In contrast, when opposite twists are used in warp and weft (Z × S), a very different, larger-scale pattern will appear, forming distinct undulations in the fabric surface. This texture emerges because, when Z and S yarns cross one another, nesting is prevented, allowing more freedom of yarn movement. Also, since the warp and weft yarns are spiralling in different directions, these spirals are able to 'fit in' with one another. In a fabric with opposite twists, the S yarns can be observed forming S spirals, while the Z yarns form Z spirals, and it can be clearly seen that these do not impede one another.

The pictures show tracking and undulation patterns produced by industrial crepe wool yarns and can be regarded as

fairly typical, but these textures vary considerably. Not surprisingly, the dominant factor is the amount of yarn twist, with the textures appearing only faintly, if at all, with low-twist yarns and becoming progressively stronger with increasing amounts of twist. However, the tracking and undulating patterns tend to emerge at slightly different levels of twist. Tracking often occurs with yarns that are only slightly unbalanced, and it will then simply create the illusion of a diamond twill in an otherwise flat fabric. With higher levels of twist, a certain amount of fabric buckling tends to occur in addition to the 'twill' lines.

Z and S interactions behave differently; yarns that are only slightly unbalanced will usually not produce any texture at all. The fact that the yarns push away from one another (as nesting is prevented) simply gives a fuller handle to the fabric. As twist levels rise, the undulating pattern gradually begins to appear, becoming very striking in the case of extremely

With very open setts the same-twist and opposite-twist patterns become less clearly differentiated from one another, though the Z × S undulations always remain more regular than the bubbled textures produced by same-twist interactions. Crepe wool 27/1 Nm, 24 epi, ppi.

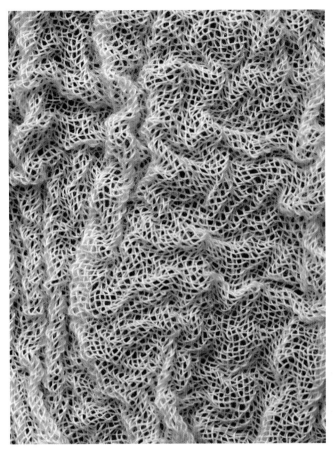

Warp and weft: S twist.

Warp: S twist. Weft: Z twist.

high-twist yarns, such as the industrial crepes shown here. However, although the amount of twist is very important in producing these effects, other factors — sett, fibre, type of spin and weave structure — also influence the patterns of texture.

Influence of Sett

Variations in sett will affect the form and distinctness of the tracking and undulation textures. In general, at relatively close setts, yarn movement is restricted, and this tends to inhibit the formation of texture. As the sett is opened up, textures begin to emerge clearly. But with extremely open setts, yarn movement begins to take place so freely that definite patterns become less obvious, being gradually replaced by overall crinkly textures. There are, however, some differences

in the way that the sett influences the two different types of twist interactions.

With a close sett, and the same twist direction in warp and weft, tracking lines may appear only faintly and rather irregularly, if at all. At intermediate setts the tracking lines are regularly distributed and very clear (*see* Chapter 2 for Sharon Alderman's experiments on tracking). As the sett is further opened up, the lines become less sharp, as the yarns move more freely and distribute their energy evenly throughout the structure, and an irregular bubbly texture may begin to emerge, especially with very high-twist yarns. A further opening up of the sett tends to result in an overall crinkly texture.

In the case of Z and S interactions, if the sett is very open, the undulating texture takes the form of tightly curled waves. At intermediate setts the undulations become more bold and regular. As the sett is closed up, yarn movement starts to become restricted and the undulating texture becomes less consistent. With very close setts the waves become subdued and irregular, breaking out here and there in a disorganized way. Sharp lines (like those of the tracking pattern) may also begin to appear in places.

So, to sum up, as the sett is *closed up* (and yarn movement is restricted), Z × S interactions will develop some of the characteristics of same-twist interactions. And, conversely, as the sett is *opened up*, (and yarn movement increased), same-twist interactions will begin to develop a more bubbly texture, though without ever achieving the very regular undulations of Z × S interactions. These variations are consistent with the general principle that tracking patterns depend on a partial *restriction of yarn movement*, while undulations depend on *free yarn movement*.

Clearly, for any particular yarn there will be a fairly narrow range of setts that will allow the characteristic tracking and undulating patterns to form in the most distinctive ways. It is also worth remembering that a slightly lower sett is desirable for the optimum effect with undulations than is the case for tracking, given that free movement is so important for Z and S interactions. This naturally has implications for combining these different textures within a design.

Influence of Fibre and Type of Spin on Fabric Texture

Textile fibres vary greatly in their basic physical properties, and different spinning methods align the fibres to a greater or lesser extent, further affecting these properties in the finished yarn. Two particularly important factors are the stiffness and the compactness of the yarn. These characteristics can reinforce one another to give a particularly strong stress response, which results in very definite textures. Since fibre stiffness increases with fibre diameter, thicker fibres readily produce stiffer yarns, which respond to stress more strongly than yarns of a similar thickness that are made from finer fibres. This reaction is further enhanced by good fibre alignment, which tends to produce a more compact yarn that is likely to give a stronger stress response than a softer, more airy yarn. A stiff yarn that does not bend easily will also naturally tend to form a larger scale spiral in response to stress than a softer yarn.

These factors can be best understood by considering the different character of worsted spun and woollen spun yarns.

From the outset, the various breeds of sheep produce fibres of different diameter, length and other characteristics, which are suitable for different types of yarn, but these inherent properties of the fibres can be further enhanced by different methods of fibre preparation and spinning. Typically, in worsted spinning, long, fairly large-diameter, stiff fibres are processed to give excellent alignment, resulting in a compact, stiff yarn. In contrast, woollen yarns are prepared from shorter, finer fibres, which are not strongly aligned, producing a softer, more airy structure. But even when worsted yarns are made from fine fibres, the alignment of these fibres means that the yarn will behave differently from a woollen yarn prepared with fibres of a similar thickness.

The characteristics of these different types of yarn become very obvious when they are highly twisted. Worsted yarns begin to create textures at much lower levels of twist than woollen yarns, and the patterns are also slightly different. Stiff worsted yarns tend to form large-scale spirals, while softer woollen yarns are able to bend more easily and form smaller-scale spirals (in relation to the thickness of the yarn). These differences impact on both the tracking and undulating patterns described above, so that woollen yarns generally produce textures that are less bold and crisp than those of worsted yarns.

With same-twist interactions, woollen yarns tend to produce an overall crinkled effect, especially with very open setts. As the sett is made a little closer, tracking lines will begin to appear, but these are not as clear and crisp as those produced by worsted yarns. With opposite-twist interactions, an undulating pattern may emerge, especially at very high levels of twist, but this texture is likely to have a softer appearance than with worsted yarns and to be smaller in scale, relative to the yarn thickness.

These differences mean that woollen and worsted yarns have different virtues in the design of textured fabrics. Worsted yarns, such as industrial crepes, are particularly good for producing crisp surface textures in simple weaves, while woollen yarns tend to produce a softer, more crinkly texture and are also excellent for float weaves where good shrinkage is important (*see* Chapter 5). These principles, of yarn character, scale of spiral and suitability for different purposes, also apply to yarns made from other fibres such as silk and cotton. However, though useful as a rule of thumb, such categorization does simplify the situation, since many different combinations of yarns may produce successful designs. The question of the scale of spiral produced by a yarn, *in relation to its thickness*, is especially interesting. A fine, stiff yarn may

Textural patterns in 2/2 twill. Crepe wool 58/2 Nm, 32 epi, ppi.

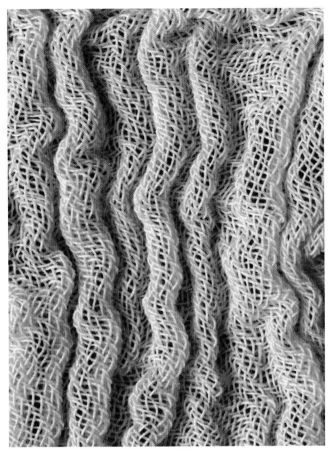

Warp and weft: Z twist.

Warp: Z twist. Weft: S twist.

end up making a spiral of a similar size to that produced by a much thicker, but softer yarn, so there is scope for 'matching up' unexpected partners to create fabrics with interesting mixed properties of handle and texture.

Influence of Weave Structure

Tracking and undulation patterns are also influenced by weave structure. For example, compared with plain weave, twill weaves allow greater yarn movement within the fabric, and this, of course, influences both same-twist and opposite-twist yarn interactions. The undulating texture produced with Z × S yarns can be enhanced by the increased opportunities for yarn movement, so that it becomes more regular and consistent.

In contrast, when twill is used with same-twist yarn interactions, the tracking effect tends to be subdued, as some of

the surplus yarn energy is dissipated through the more flexible structure of the weave. With moderately twisted yarns, the tracking effect may be completely lost. On the other hand, with very high-twist yarns (like the industrial crepes shown here) there is generally so much surplus energy that, although sharp tracking lines no longer appear, they are replaced by an irregular, slightly wavy texture.

Weave structure does, of course, also interact with the properties of yarns and fibres. The patterns shown here are typical of those produced by high-twist worsted yarns. However, as already mentioned, softer woollen yarns tend to react differently. In the case of these more tightly crinkling yarns, the dissipation of energy in a twill weave may result in much less distinct textures than those produced in plain weave, not only for same-twist tracking patterns, but also for opposite-twist undulations. However, the influence of sett will also play a part in controlling the amount of yarn movement that can take place.

51

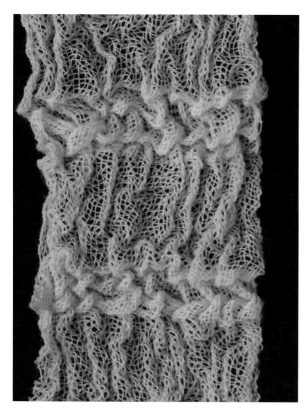

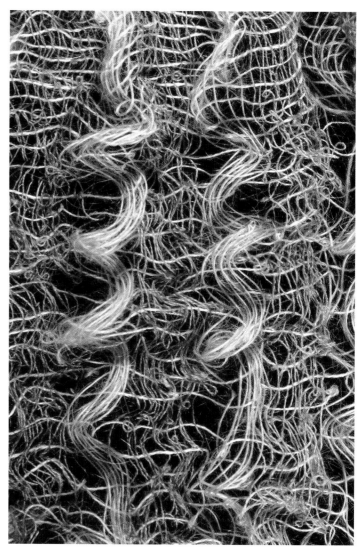

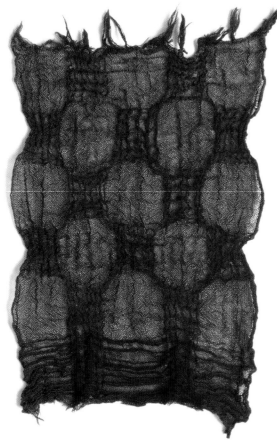

ABOVE LEFT:
Weftways stripes of Z and S yarns create narrow bands of same-twist and opposite-twist textures, in plain weave. Warp: Crepe wool 27.5/1 Nm, Z twist, 24 epi. Weft: Crepe wool 27.5/1 Nm, Z twist, 24 ppi and wool 2/60 w.c. (S twist), 28 ppi.

ABOVE:
In this very lightly beaten fabric by Mary Frame, warp yarns that differ in both character and direction of twist, behave very differently. A thick Z-twist singles is stiff enough to form a large-scale spiral and also has the opposite twist to the weft. These yarns spiral together, producing a Z-ringlet – a dramatic version of the undulating texture, made possible by the extremely open sett. In contrast, the finer S-ply yarns, which have the same twist direction as the weft, produce a more subdued texture. (Photo: Carol Sawyer)

LEFT:
Sample of plain weave fabric in which stripes of Z and S yarns have been used in both warp and weft. Curves emerge from the chequerboard of same-twist and opposite-twist textures. Warp and weft: Crepe wool 30/1 Nm, 32 epi, ppi.

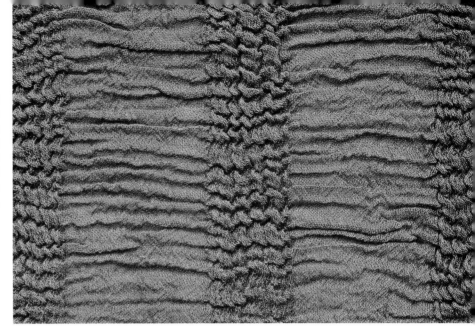

Sample in which stripes of different twist are combined with variations in structure. The undulating texture emerges where Z and S yarns cross one another in 2/2 twill, while the less textured stripes result from Z yarns crossing one another in plain weave. Warp: Crepe wool 58/2 Nm, Z and S, 30 epi. Weft: High-twist cotton 34 Nm, 35 ppi.

Stripes of Z and S twist yarns in both warp and weft create a chequerboard of same-twist and opposite-twist interactions. Same-twist blocks are in plain weave and they show a combination of fabric buckling and tracking lines. The opposite-twist blocks are in 2/2 twill and these have developed an undulating texture. Warp: Crepe wool 58/2 Nm, Z and S, 30 epi, 30 ppi.

Combining Tracking and Undulations

As well as producing all-over textures, the different twist interactions can be used to create simple designs based on texture variations within the fabric, by using stripes of Z and S yarns in either the warp or weft, or in both. These will intersect to give stripes or blocks of same-twist and opposite-twist textures. Many different effects are possible depending on the character of the yarn, the width of the stripes and the sett. The undulating texture causes more fabric contraction than the tracking effect, so interesting curves can emerge from the blocks of different textures.

As mentioned earlier, the sett that is desirable for producing the best undulations tends to be slightly lower than that which gives the clearest tracking effect. A good solution is to vary the structure so that the same-twist blocks are plain weave, while the Z × S blocks are twill. This gives more space for the yarns (effectively reducing the sett) and also takes advantage of the fact that tracking shows up best in plain weave and undulations show up best in twill. There are further possibilities for creating textural variations by combining yarns of different character or thickness, and/or with different amounts of twist. For example, refer to the article by Dorothy Cross in the Jan/Feb 2003 issue of *Handwoven*, in which she uses stripes of Z crepe wool and S-plied merino wool, in both warp and weft (*see* Bibliography).

53

More About Tracking

Tracking patterns are easily produced, often accidentally, when using yarns that are not really 'high-twist' at all, and so it is worth trying to understand more about how they arise. Tracking lines appear to start and stop spontaneously, and they vary in length and prominence in different fabrics, depending on the character and twist of the warp and weft yarns. If warp and weft are of the same material, with similar amounts of twist, then the tracking lines are equally prominent in both directions and tend to be short in length. Since the twist direction is the same in both warp and weft, yarn nesting is probably occurring (*see* Chapter 1), which restricts yarn movement so that yarns cannot curl completely freely.

However, all yarns vary a little in twist along their length, and there must be places where a yarn is so highly twisted that it can curl more strongly than usual and so become displaced from its vertical position. It is easy to visualize how such a displacement would make space to allow the adjacent thread to curl in a similar way at the next intersection, setting off a sequence of curling threads that runs down the fabric. As a succession of threads curl in this way, they tend to fall against one another forming a continuous diagonal line, running in the *same* direction as the yarn twist. In a Z × Z fabric, if the fabric is viewed with the warp running vertically, diagonal Z-lines are formed where adjacent warp threads curl in a Z direction, while lines running in an S direction are formed by the weft. These weft yarns are, of course, also really curling in a Z direction, and this can be easily seen if the fabric is turned so that the weft runs vertically. The reverse is true for an S × S fabric, where the yarns in both directions curl in an S direction. The overall visual effect of this tracking is similar in both cases, though the subtle difference between Z × Z and S × S cloths can be seen if the fabric is examined closely, especially if the warp and weft are of different colours.

These diagonal lines, precisely related to twist direction, emerge very clearly with high-twist yarns in a balanced plain weave (that is, with the same sett in both warp and weft). Yarns that are only moderately twisted tend to create a more variable effect, and may sometimes give an impression of lines running both with and against the twist direction of the yarn. However, a close look at such a fabric shows that the yarns are *still curling* in the same direction as their twist. It is simply that, particularly with less forceful yarns, lines running in the opposite direction to the twist also start to become visible under some circumstances. For example, if warp and weft are of strongly contrasting colours, the paler or brighter yarn will usually be seen more clearly. Differences in the sett of warp and weft are also relevant, because as yarns are pushed more closely together, this produces an apparently contradictory result: although the yarns are still curling in the *same* direction as their twist, the eye begins to pick up a line running in the *opposite* direction.

The influence of sett can be seen very clearly in plain-weave cloths that are strongly warp- or weft-faced. An impression is given of a faint twill line running throughout the fabric in the opposite direction to the yarn twist (that is, a Z-twist yarn will appear to create an S-twill effect). The line is reversed if the direction of the yarn twist is changed, and such twist reversals can produce an effect reminiscent of a herringbone twill. This provides one of the earliest examples of the exploitation of yarn twist to create a visual effect in a textile, since it was known as far back as the Bronze Age (*see* Chapter 2).

Preventing Tracking

Tracking effects often appear with yarns that are only slightly unbalanced, and many weavers are familiar with such, sometimes unwanted, textures. Of course, this is a book about *producing* texture, and tracking is considered here mainly in terms of its charming appearance and potential for design! But understanding how to create and use an effect can also give the power to eliminate it, should that be desired. Tracking may occur not only with single yarns (which will obviously be unbalanced), but also sometimes with plied yarns (which have often been slightly 'over-plied' and so may not be perfectly balanced). Worsted yarns are particularly prone to tracking, because their stiffness means that they readily respond to the small amount of stress that results from a very slight lack of balance.

As noted above, when working with yarns that are only slightly unbalanced, changing from plain weave to twill will often completely avoid unwanted tracking effects, by allowing the small amount of surplus yarn energy to be dissipated through the more flexible structure of the twill. Alternatively, if a plain weave fabric is required, changing either the warp or the weft to the opposite twist can remove the tracking effect. In the case of worsteds, these yarns are normally plied S, so this will generally mean substituting a singles yarn (these are normally Z twist) for either warp or weft. This should be a low-twist yarn, to avoid the risk of an undulating texture emerging, particularly if working with a very open sett.

TWIST-TWILL INTERACTIONS

The way 'twill-effect' lines appear in warp- or weft-faced plain-weave fabrics is probably related to the phenomenon of twist-twill interactions. Just as yarns can be twisted to the left (S) or the right (Z), the diagonal lines of twills can incline to the left or right, and the symbols S and Z are also used in this case. If the line of a twill runs in the *opposite* direction to the yarn twist, then the twill line becomes very distinct, as compared with when the yarn twist and twill line are the same, when the twill line becomes more subdued. It is worth being aware of these interactions, so that you can choose whether or not to emphasize the twill line. These effects can be clearly seen in fabrics where the twill line reverses to form the design, while the direction of the yarn twist remains the same – for example, herringbone twills. If these fabrics are examined closely, it will be seen that the twill line is clearer in one direction than the other. Similar principles apply in the case of satins: although these weaves are designed to create a uniform surface, there is usually a slight tendency for a twill line to be visible. Robinson and Marks in *Woven Cloth Construction* (*see* Bibliography) give a detailed account of twist-twill interactions.

However, although these effects can be very clearly seen with 'normal' yarns, this principle breaks down in the case of very high-twist yarns, such as industrial crepes. The tracking and undulation patterns that have already been described exert a more powerful influence and cause the twist and twill effects to reinforce one another. Distinct twill lines then emerge when the twist and twill directions are the same.

Setting the fabric, using appropriate heat treatments such as crabbing, can also eliminate tracking – for this process refer to *The Craft of the Weaver* by Ann Sutton *et al* pp. 100-103 (*see* Bibliography). Sharon Alderman told me about an interesting way to set the fabric, which she discovered by accident. She placed a fabric in hot water and was then called away, so that it was left untouched in the water. Later, when the water had become completely cold, she found that the fabric had become set and no longer developed a tracking pattern when washed. She has adopted this as a finishing method when she wishes to avoid tracking, and has found that it is very important to avoid any disturbance of the fabric, as the slightest input of energy through touching it can trigger the tracking response. In contrast, if she wishes to use the tracking effect as part of the design, she will handle the fabric vigorously during finishing. When working with very high-twist yarns it is also sometimes necessary to agitate a fabric in order to provoke the creping response (*see* Chapter 8).

Other Fibres

So far the examples have been mainly concerned with wool. Although wool responds particularly well to high levels of twist, the stress reaction responsible for these yarn movements also occurs with other fibres that swell on wetting and which have suitable elastic properties. The main fibres used for the production of crepe yarns are cotton, rayon (made from reconstituted cellulose) and silk. Bast fibres, such as linen, also show a reaction but tend to create a less springy texture, probably due to their lack of elasticity. Paper yarns, if produced as a single strand, are also unbalanced, and can create very interesting textured effects. Christina Leitner (2005) gives an excellent and very detailed account of the possibilities of paper yarns (*see* Bibliography). Synthetics are not satisfactory for producing high-twist yarns, since they do not swell very much on wetting, though synthetic shrink yarns, constructed on quite different principles, are now widely used (*see* Chapter 9).

Opening Up the Possibilities in Simple Weaves

The examples so far have shown the effects of using high-twist yarns in both warp and weft. But some of the most interesting and successful designs are only partly dependent on very high-twist yarns, because they also include other yarns that are lower-twist or balanced. These different types of yarn may be thought of as 'active' and 'passive'.

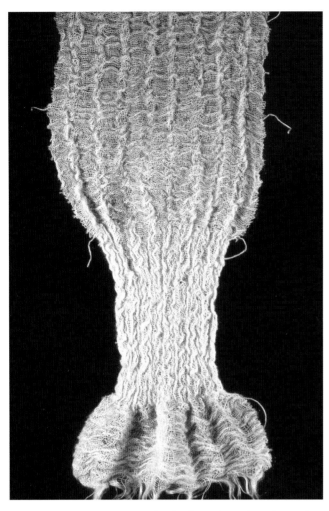

This sample by Mary Frame clearly shows how the *relationship* between warp and weft determines the way that texture develops within a fabric. The warp is the same throughout, but appears to be active or passive depending on whether it is crossed by a weft that is more or less active than itself (refer to Mary Frame's 'Ringlets and Waves: Undulations from Overtwist' – *see* Bibliography). (Photo: Carol Sawyer)

'Active' and 'Passive' Yarns

It seems natural to think of strongly unbalanced yarns as 'active', since their spiral movements actively create texture in the fabric. In contrast, balanced, normal-twist yarns seem 'passive', since they create a texture when they are *pushed* by the 'active' yarns. Of course, no fibre or yarn is truly 'passive' in an ultimate sense, since they all impart some physi-

cal character to the finished fabric. But this distinction can be quite useful when trying to visualize a design, and a variety of examples are given below of ways in which different combinations of 'active' and 'passive' yarns can create texture.

However, it is important to remember that the development of texture depends not only on the *absolute* characteristics of the yarns, but also on the *relation* between the properties of yarns in different parts of the fabric. Yarns range in character from wildly 'active' crepes to yarns that are perfectly balanced, and many yarns that fall between these extremes may behave in an active or a passive way, depending on the context. For example, a warp may show warpways or weftways shrinkage along its length, depending on the properties of the wefts that are laid across it, as can be clearly seen in a beautiful sample by Mary Frame. The warp is the same throughout, but appears active or passive depending on the context. So, as well as regarding a yarn as highly active or relatively passive in terms of its inherent properties, it is also important to consider whether it is playing an active or passive *role* in a particular design or part of a design.

PASSIVE WARPS AND ACTIVE WEFTS (AND VICE VERSA)

One of the most common ways of combining passive and active yarns is to use a relatively balanced yarn in the warp and a high-twist yarn in the weft. This arrangement is widely used both in handweaving and in industry, because crepe yarns can be rather lively to handle and this tends to make warping difficult. A wide variety of textures can be achieved in this way, by varying fibre, yarn twist and sett.

However, the extra care needed for warping with high-twist yarns can be very worthwhile. For example, scarves and shawls can be made that are stretchy along their length, which makes an attractive and comfortable fabric for wrapping around the body. In the case of garments, if these are woven 'sideways', with the intention that the weft will run vertically in the finished item, then the selvedges can make neat edges that do not need hemming.

In all cases, when finishing such fabrics, it is helpful to encourage the yarn crimp to migrate to either the warp or weft (whichever element is expected to contract) by pulling hard in the opposite direction: thus with a normal-twist warp and high-twist weft, pull in the warp direction. This process of 'crimp interchange' tends to transfer the yarn crimp mainly to the contracting element, pushing it slightly out of the cloth where it has more scope for movement and shrinkage.

This twill scarf by Sheila Reimann (New Zealand) has a high-twist wool warp and a weft of spun silk. This combination of active warp and passive weft gives a beautiful springy quality to the fabric along its length.

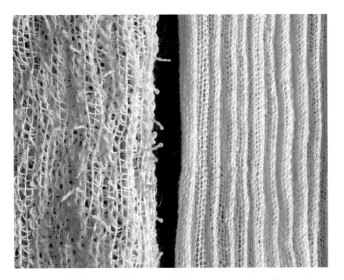

Left: A widely spaced warp will allow twists of weft yarn to project from the fabric. Warp: Linen 44 lea, 12 epi. Weft: Crepe wool 27.5/1 Nm, 24 ppi. *Right*: With a closer sett, the high-twist yarn distorts the fabric itself, giving a crepon texture. Warp: Linen 44 lea, 32 epi. Weft: Crepe wool 27/1 Nm, 32 ppi.

The Influence of Sett:
Bouclé and Crepon

When working with high-twist weft on a normal-twist warp, different textures will be produced according to the sett of the warp. With a very open sett, a high-twist weft may be able to release some of its energy by escaping between the widely spaced warp yarns and plying back on itself, forming small twisted loops that project from the surface of the fabric. This can often produce a rather untidy effect and could be thought of as a fault. However, when pushed to extremes, a certain degree of consistency can develop, creating a kind of bouclé texture. Junichi Arai uses this very effectively in some of his multiple layer cloths (*see* Chapters 6 and 7).

As the sett is increased, the weft is less able to escape in this way, so that the yarn movements also begin to disturb the surface of the cloth. Finally, a stage is reached where the spiral course of the weft definitely takes the fabric with it, forming an irregular, softly pleated effect known as crepon. Innumerable variations of this pleated texture are possible, depending on fibre, yarn twist and sett, and a wide range of different combinations of materials and yarn thickness can be successful (*see* Chapter 10). This is one of the most adaptable techniques, perhaps because of its inherent simplicity. High-twist yarns vary so much in character, and the range of normal-twist yarns available is so wide, that the possibilities for subtly different textures and cloth qualities seem endless. This attractive texture also combines well with other structures.

LEFT:
A wrap from the 'Twist' series by Liz Williamson (Australia), woven in wool and high-twist wool. (Photo: Ian Hobbs)

OPPOSITE:
This bold design by Junichi Arai depends on the interplay of several elements. Alternating yarns of black and white (normal-twist in the warp and high-twist in the weft) create a crepon texture with different colour-and-weave effects on the two sides. Blocks of unwoven warp make a dramatic contrast to this fine texture. These grade from white to black because the last pick of a woven section raises all the white ends, while the first pick of the next woven section lifts all the black ends. Arai excels at creating striking effects by subtle and simple means. (Ann Sutton Collection)

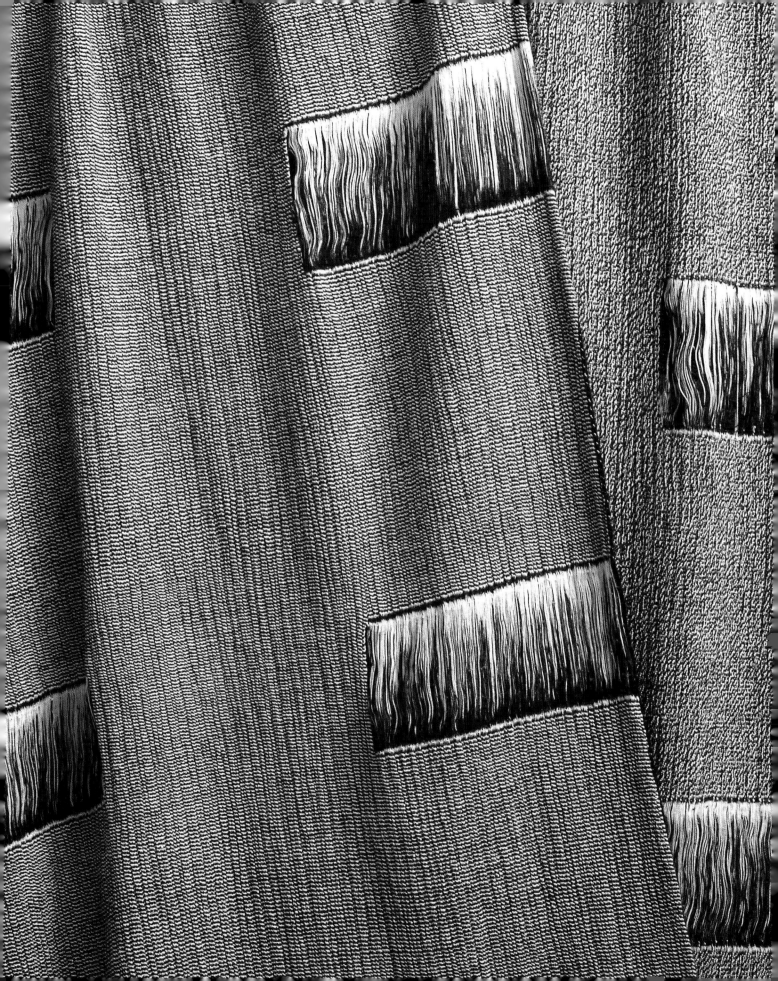

Reversals of twist direction create a discontinuity in the cloth. Warp: Linen 44 lea, 32 epi. Weft: Crepe wool 27/1 Nm 32 ppi.

The Influence of Twist Direction: Crepon and Crepe

The crepon effect can be produced using either Z or S yarn as weft. However, yarns of these different twists will spiral in different directions as they form the pleating. If the warp is perfectly balanced, then the direction of weft twist should not make any difference to the general effect in the fabric. However, few yarns, even plied ones, are quite perfectly balanced, so it is useful to remember that using opposite twists in warp and weft increases yarn movement. If the warp is moderately unbalanced, this can produce a wavy crepon as the S × Z undulations (described above) come into play, and it can become an interesting aspect of the design. However, if

the warp is only slightly unbalanced, the use of an opposite twist weft may simply encourage fabric curling, where the corners of the fabric flick over in an annoying way. So, as a rule of thumb, when using a warp that is not unbalanced enough to create interesting undulations within the fabric, it may be helpful to choose a crepe yarn that is the *same* direction of twist as the warp, in order to reduce fabric curling at the corners.

When weaving a crepon fabric, if the weft is changed from Z to S, this will be visible as a faint line in the fabric, as the yarns at this junction 'fight' one another in their attempt to spiral in different directions. Simply reversing the twists in this way, at intervals of a few centimetres, can make an attractive, simple design in itself. Fabric curling is not normally much of a problem in this case, although it is usually wise to finish the fabric with bands of weft that are the same twist as the warp, to reduce curling at the corners of the cloth.

The smaller the interval between reversals of twist direction, the greater the extent to which the different twists will work against one another and the crepon effect gradually breaks down. With very frequent twist reversals, the pleating effect disappears, to be replaced by an all-over crinkled texture – the classic *crepe* fabric (2S, 2Z is the usual arrangement). Although it is very common to produce the crepe effect in this way, with a passive warp, crepe fabrics are also sometimes manufactured using crepe yarns and twist reversals in both warp and weft.

It is also possible to produce a 'quick crepe', which has a somewhat subdued texture, by winding a Z and an S yarn together on the same bobbin. This works particularly well with silk crepes, but the bobbins need to be wound very carefully to avoid tangling, especially with the very finest yarns. A better solution is to use an end-delivery shuttle lined with fur (*see* Chapter 8), which controls the release of the yarn.

OPPOSITE:
A series of samples, showing Z and S twist reversals after different numbers of picks. *Top left*: 24S, 24Z. *Top right*: 12S, 12Z. *Bottom left*: 6S, 6Z. *Bottom right*: 2S, 2Z. With frequent reversals the different twists work against one another, producing crepe rather than crepon. This also has the effect of restricting yarn contraction, so as reversals become more frequent, the samples become wider. Warp: Spun silk 60/2 Nm, 28 epi. Weft: Crepe wool 30/1 Nm, 30 ppi.

Lotte Dalgaard subtly contrasts the effect of lambswool and crepe wool warps in this twill fabric. The weft is crepe wool. An undulating texture emerges where the crepe yarns cross one another but is prevented by the thicker, more softly twisted lambswool. (Photo: Ole Akhøj)

Varying the Sett

Since sett is so critical in determining the exact result obtained with high-twist yarns, it is not surprising that varying the sett and/or the yarn thickness within the fabric, in either warp or weft or both, can create interesting effects by allowing different textures to emerge. Where yarns are very closely packed or are relatively thick, no texture will appear, and these flat areas can be played off against more openly set areas of the fabric where texture can emerge freely.

It can also be effective to carry things to extremes by alternating densely crammed areas with gaps in the fabric, where the high-twist yarns can relax completely freely, creating lines of a crinkled texture along the fabric.

Mixing Active and Passive Yarns in the Weft (or Warp)

So far, the examples of active/passive combinations have simply involved normal yarns in one direction with high-twist yarns in the other. But particularly strong textures can be produced by using combinations of these different types of yarn in either the warp or weft direction, or both. A simple weft stripe arrangement of high-twist and normal yarns can create seersucker effects. This is a case where an intuitive sense of the yarns being active and passive emerges very strongly, as it becomes obvious that the high-twist yarn is actively *pushing* the passive one into interesting distortions.

TOP LEFT:
Seersucker sample, with weft stripes in spun silk and crepe wool/crepe silk. The use of black and white yarns in both warp and weft creates colour-and-weave effects. Warp: Spun silk 60/2 Nm, 32 epi. Weft: Spun silk 30/2 Nm, 28 ppi, crepe wool 50/2 Nm and crepe silk 4 × 40/44 denier (alternate picks), 36 ppi.

BOTTOM LEFT:
This Japanese silk crepe kimono fabric includes a weftways seersucker stripe produced by introducing a normal-twist yarn in place of the crepe weft in parts of the fabric. An additional, lightly twisted yarn is also used to float on the surface to create a glossy, brightly coloured spot, which contrasts with the matt texture of the crepe. (Designer unknown. Gift from Sheila Reimann)

OPPOSITE:
These two fabrics by the Nuno Corporation are woven with an interesting combination of thick/thin and active/passive yarns. The warp yarns are normal twist – a very fine yarn, together with paired ends of a heavier yarn. The weft is mainly woven from the same fine yarn as in the warp, to create an almost transparent fabric. This is thrown into a crepon texture by paired picks of a thicker high-twist yarn (top left). On the right, this texture is contrasted with weftways stripes of normal yarn, creating a seersucker effect.

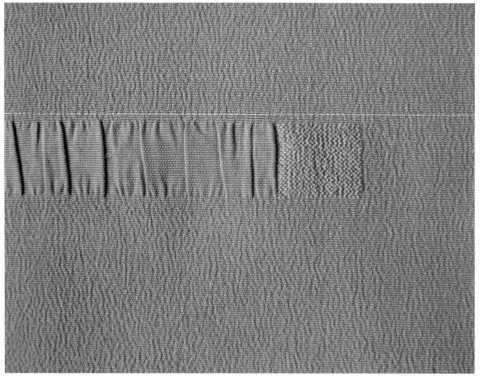

A weftways seersucker stripe produced through the contrast between linen and high-twist wool. Warp: Spun silk 60/2 Nm, 32 epi. Weft: Linen 30 lea, 28 ppi, crepe wool 50/2 Nm, 32 ppi.

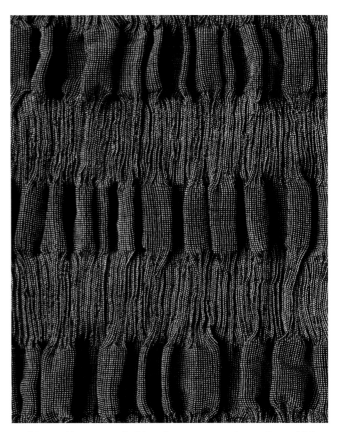

This scarf has a very bold weftways seersucker stripe, which results from the strong contrast between a stiff mohair yarn and high-twist wool.

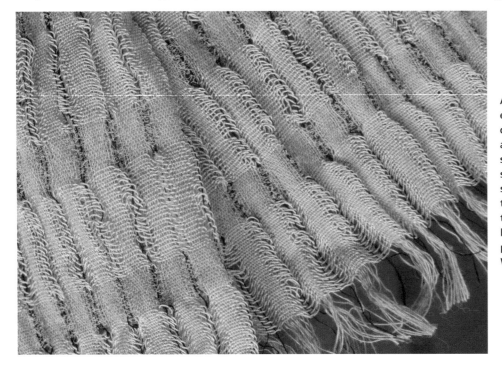

A scarf that emphasizes the effect of contrasting materials by combining them with cramming and spacing. Weft stripes of crepe silk alternate with stripes of spun silk. The contraction of the crepe silk is so strong that the gaps in the fabric almost disappear, and the texture is actually created by loops of spun silk, which are being passively displaced. Warp: Linen. Weft: Spun silk and crepe silk.

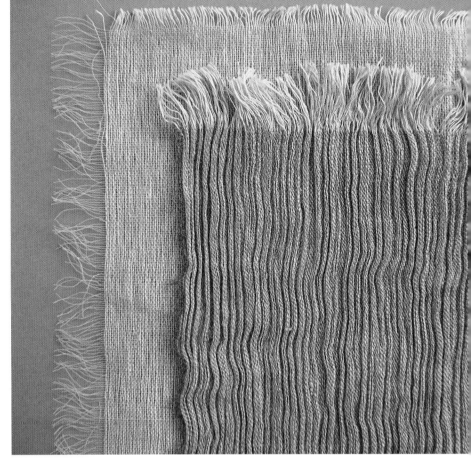

The linen warp for this crepon fabric was dyed with Procion dyes. The fabric was woven with an undyed crepe silk weft, and the piece was subsequently piece-dyed with a dyestuff that had an affinity only for the silk yarn. A sample of the fabric, after weaving but before finishing, can be seen in the background. Some warp threads have been removed so that the undyed crepe silk wefts can be seen projecting from the left-hand edge of the fabric. The finished fabric, after washing and dyeing, is in the foreground. The crepe weft, now with a crinkly texture and dyed red, can be seen at the edge of the cloth.

The same principle can be pushed even further by using materials with properties that contrast very strongly with the high-twist yarn. A normal-twist yarn of silk or cotton can provide a foil to a high-twist yarn, but a linen yarn, because of its stiffness and lack of elasticity, will produce an even stronger contrast. However, some care is needed here. Fine linen yarns are likely to work very well in this situation, but a thicker yarn might prove too stiff and prevent any texture forming at all. So how thick is too thick? This is exactly the type of question that you can only answer by sampling. Every situation will be different, depending on the other yarns involved and the sett. Contrasts of this type, between high-twist and normal yarns, can also be combined with cramming and spacing.

Piece-Dyeing and Cross-Dyeing

The first time a high-twist yarn is wetted out, it shows the creping reaction. Once this has happened, the yarn will not react so strongly again in subsequent washes – it is as though it has lost some of its energy. This may be partly due to the relaxation of the fibres that has taken place, but the fact that many yarns are softened by the first wash may also be relevant, since softer yarns tend to give a weaker stress response than stiff ones. In many designs, all the available energy and stiffness in a yarn may be needed to get a desired effect, so it is necessary to avoid wetting out the yarn before weaving. This obviously limits the possibilities for dyeing yarns.

This can be a problem because many commercial crepe yarns are undyed. Traditionally, the normal practice in industry has been to weave crepe fabrics with undyed yarns and then dye the finished cloth (piece-dyeing). The situation has improved recently, since a good range of coloured yarns has become available from Japan, especially wool crepes, which are produced by dyeing the fibres before spinning. However, some types of crepe yarns, especially silks, are still usually available undyed. When working with these, it is possible to introduce colour by emulating the industrial process of piece-dyeing. A range of related colours can be applied through careful planning, to take advantage of the way that successive colour applications blend. For example, a red warp could be crossed with an undyed high-twist weft and the fabric could then be dyed blue, to produce a purple warp with a blue weft.

Even greater possibilities are offered by mixing dyes of animal and vegetable origin, since contrasts of colour can be achieved when the yarns have affinities for different dyestuffs. They can then be dyed in a two-stage process of *cross-*

dyeing. For example, if cotton, linen or rayon yarns are dyed with Procions (fibre-reactive dyes with an affinity for cellulose fibres) and woven with undyed yarns of wool or silk, then the finished cloth can be immersed in a dye which takes only on protein fibres (for example acid dyes, metal complex dyes). It is possible to get a wide variety of colour contrasts, including beautiful 'shot' effects in this way. In the process, the vegetable fibres may be coloured slightly by the wool/silk dyes, especially if dark colours are being applied, but the dye does not really bond properly to vegetable fibres and can be removed from them by simmering the fabric in a mild detergent for a few minutes. There will then be a clear contrast between the colours of the animal and vegetable fibres.

Cross-dyeing can also be applied to a completely undyed cloth, using successive dyebaths for the different fibres, which is the normal process in industry. But for the hand weaver, dyeing some of the yarn before weaving obviously gives the possibility of greater colour control and subtler effects. More information about piece-dyeing and cross-dyeing is given in Chapter 8.

Gauze

Gauze involves a special weaving technique in which adjacent warp ends cross over one another, between successive picks. This structure holds the weft yarn very firmly in position, so it is possible to use very open setts and yet still produce a stable fabric, in a way that would not be possible with a normal plain weave. Many of the general principles already described can be successfully applied to this structure, but with the difference that yarns have more scope for movement in this open weave. The crossed warps of the gauze structure can be achieved either with special half-heddles, called *doups,* or with beads. Both systems work well, but the doups have to be specially made, which is quite a time-consuming process, so the system with beads is quicker to set up, and this is the method described here.

Setting up a Gauze Warp

When setting up a gauze warp for the first time, it can be helpful to warp with three colours, since this makes it easier to keep track of the threading. The contrasting colours also make an interesting effect within the weave structure.

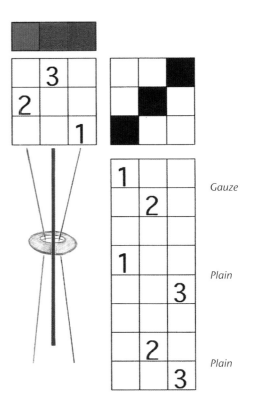

The crossing of the warp threads is produced by alternately raising shafts 1 and 2. When shaft 1 is raised, the whip threads will rise on one side of the ground thread (shown in red) and then, when shaft 2 is raised, the whip threads will come up on the other side. Plain weave can also be woven with this set-up by alternately raising either shaft 1 or 2 and the ground thread. Although only three shafts are necessary, in practice it is helpful to put the ground thread (shown on shaft 3) on the very back shaft of the loom, to minimize stress on the threads when they cross.

Gauze set-up: First thread the warp through the heddles, as shown on the draft, assigning each colour to its correct shaft. The next stage is to thread the beads. The red ends are *ground threads* and will remain down during gauze weaving: these do not pass through a bead. The green and blue ends are *whip threads* and will rise to make the crossed structure: these are joined with a bead so that they act as one thread. It is best to avoid using large, round beads, as they tend to jam against one another. Small beads work well, but they are fiddly to handle and tend to have very small holes that are difficult to thread (a needle threader is useful for this). A good compromise is to look for medium-sized beads that have a flat, disc-like shape, since their bevelled edges allow them to slip past one another without jamming and they usually have holes of moderate size.

Treat each unit of three ends in this way: Take one of the whip threads, pass it *under* the red ground thread, and then pull both the whip threads together through a bead. So you should finish up with the two whip threads passing *through* the bead and the red ground thread passing *over* the bead. Tie the three threads together with a slip knot so that the bead cannot fall off. When all the gauze units have been threaded, take each unit of three ends and thread it through a single reed dent. *All three threads must be in one dent for crossing to take place.* A sett of about two units/cm (five units/inch) will make quite an open cloth suitable for your first experiments. Any reed can be used – simply leave empty dents as necessary.

Alternatively, if you make a reasonably wide warp, you might choose to vary the sett of the gauze units across the warp to see the effect of different yarn densities. If the same yarn is used throughout, then the combined whip threads obviously give the effect of a yarn that is thicker than the ground thread. For a more consistent effect, a finer yarn can be used for the whip threads, or the ground thread could be doubled.

A note of warning: you will find that the shed produced by the gauze crossing is very shallow. It is worth acquiring a shuttle with a very low profile to use in this situation – Handweavers Studio (*see* Suppliers list) have some suitable ones.

Designing with Gauze

The main advantage of gauze is that it can produce a very open structure that is also stable, so it is ideal for allowing high-twist yarns to contract and spiral freely. Various effects can be produced using different types of high-twist yarns, and combinations of high and normal twist yarns. Woollen spun yarns tend to spiral tightly giving an overall crinkled effect. Worsted spun yarns, with their greater stiffness and tendency to form larger spirals, may produce crepons, though yarns that are extremely highly twisted (such as industrial crepe wools) often show a tendency to escape between gauze units in places, so releasing some of their energy as bouclé loops. Individual yarns will vary, so it is important to experiment. The fact that the movements made by high-twist yarns are indeed *spirals* (rather than simply up-and-down movements) has already been emphasized. These spiral movements are very evident in the gauze pleat scarf shown here, because the weft stripes, which run straight across the fabric in the loom-

'Gauze Pleat' scarf. Warp: Tussah silk. Weft: Mohair.

state, come to follow a zigzag path in the finished piece.

As well as these simple overall effects, stripes of contrasting materials can be used to create seersucker effects and other distortions. Because of the very open nature of the gauze, there is plenty of scope for dramatic effects.

The simple gauze structure described here is very well suited to work with high-twist yarns, because the yarns themselves provide plenty of interest. However, if plenty of shafts are available, additional blocks could be set up (each block requiring three shafts) so that some areas of the fabric can weave plain while others weave gauze. It is best to arrange the threading so that all the whip threads are on the front shafts while the ground threads are on the back shafts.

Gauze scarf by Noriko Matsumoto. Two different types of silk yarns are used in the warp. For the weft, the same silk yarns are plied with silk crepe yarn, to emphasize the weave structure and the texture. (Photo: Noriko Matsumoto)

A gauze piece by Fiona Crestani, exploiting the strong contrast between high-twist yarns and rusting iron wire. (Photo: Fiona Crestani)

Extreme contrasts are used to dramatic effect in this sculptural textile by Fiona Crestani (Austria). The openness of a gauze weave allows the shrinkage of high-twist yarn to be played off against the stiffness and springiness of fishing line. (Photo: Fiona Crestani)

CHAPTER 5

SUBTLE INTERPLAY: FORCEFUL FLOATS

Theory is all very well but it doesn't stop things happening.

J.M. Charcot

As explained in the last chapter, a huge range of different fabrics can be produced with simple weaves. However, further possibilities are opened up by bringing in more complex weave structures. Very strong contrasts of shrinkage can be achieved when simple structures are played off against more complex ones – plain weave, in particular, can be extremely effective as a foil to other structures. A wide variety of weaves can also create texture through their interactions with the inherent properties of different yarns. However, this chapter does not set out to give a detailed treatment of weave structure, since many excellent books on this topic already exist. Rather, the aim is to draw attention to some general principles that apply to different *types* of structure, particularly when working with high-twist yarns.

For example, some weaves tend to impose a degree of order and regularity on the high-twist yarns, while others allow a more random effect. Some constrain the movements of the yarns in certain parts of the structure and yet permit very free movement in other parts. Combining different weave structures within a fabric can also create such variations, and much of the art of working with high-twist yarns depends on getting a 'feel' for when to restrain them and when to allow them a free rein.

The precise way that individual ends and picks interlace within a structure also has implications for choosing and combining yarns. In some weaves, *all* the ends or picks spend some time weaving and some time floating (for example, Bedford cord), so any differences in shrinkage will depend on variations in the closeness or type of interlacing within the structure. In other weaves, some ends or picks are always weaving closely into the fabric, while others spend most of their time floating (for example, piqué). This immediately suggests the possibility of using normal yarns for the 'weaving' threads and high-twist yarns for the 'floating' threads, so that the properties of yarns and structures reinforce one another.

In addition to the strong textures produced by high-twist yarns, subtler effects are also noticeable once more complex weave structures come into play. Some of the contrasts of material, such as that between flexible wools or silks and stiffer linen yarns, which were discussed in the last chapter, become increasingly important when more variable structures are part of the mix. Developing an intuitive sense of how yarns and structures interact makes it possible to work with many different types of structure, freely adapting traditional weaves and creating new designs.

Warp-float and Weft-float Stripes

I am going to begin this chapter with a detailed account of one particular technique that has attracted a lot of interest

'Silk Pleat' scarf. Warp: Spun silk. Weft: Hard silk and crepe silk.

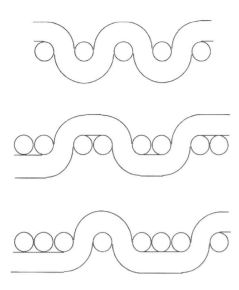

Plain weave and 2/2 twill are structures that are the same on both sides (top and middle). In 3/1 twill, the weft passes under three warp threads on one side of the fabric but over only one on the other side (bottom).

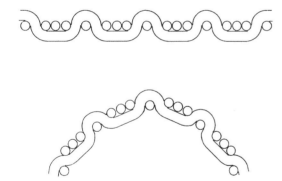

In 3/1 twill, relaxation of the three-span floats on one side of the structure causes the fabric to curl.

Using narrow stripes of 3/1 and 1/3 twill will cause the fabric to curl back and forth, creating a ribbed or pleated effect.

over the past couple of decades. This was the first textured effect that caught my attention and it remains one of my favourites. It can produce a variety of different fabric qualities, ranging from subtly ridged surfaces to deeply pleated textures, all of which have their uses. The emphasis here will be mainly on pleated textures in lightweight fabrics, since I have most experience with these, but subtler effects and heavier weights of fabric also have many possibilities. The other reason for considering this technique in some detail is that it seems to exemplify the process of working with yarns and structures: texture can be seen to *emerge* from a subtle interplay of factors. This is something that we will encounter repeatedly, with different techniques, throughout this chapter.

I have already shown a few twill fabrics in Chapter 4. These were *even* twills, with floats distributed equally on both faces of the cloth, and were used to create pattern or allow more yarn movement and texture within the fabric than would be possible with plain weave. But twills can also be *uneven*, with warp floats on one face and weft floats on the other. The cross-sectional diagrams of weave structures show how plain weave and 2/2 twill are the same on both sides, while in a 3/1 twill weft floats appear on only one side of the fabric. There are also other structures that are double-sided in a similar way.

With such double-sided fabrics, the relaxation of the floats often causes the fabric to curl. The effect is reminiscent of that seen in knitting with stocking stitch, where the relaxation of the lengthways loops on the knit side causes the top and bottom of the knitting to roll forwards, while the crossways purl loops on the back cause the sides to roll under. In weaving, in a similar way, the curling is often particularly noticeable at the edges of the cloth. Narrow stripes of the two faces of the weave can be used to make the fabric curl back and forth (rather like ribbing in knitting) to give a ridged effect that emerges from the relationships between the warp and weft yarns and the weave structure. This can vary from a faintly ribbed or embossed texture to an effect of very definite pleating, depending on the properties of the yarns, the sett and the width of the stripes. In some cases the effect may become apparent as soon as the fabric is cut from the loom, but often it is only when it is wetted out that it develops fully. The absorption of water causes fibre swelling and yarn shrinkage, which emphasizes the effect. Examples of such a fabric before and after finishing, are shown at the beginning of Chapter 1. This technique is also interesting because although it can work extremely well with unbalanced yarns (and this is how I used it initially), it does not necessarily require them.

Over the past twenty years this structure has been widely used to produce a very pronounced pleated effect, and although this is not difficult to do, the result remains somewhat unpredictable. It is far easier to define combinations of material and sett that will certainly produce the effect than to identify combinations that will fail. This is a case where theory certainly does not stop things happening, and some apparently unpromising materials may produce quite good pleating! This being so, I obviously do not expect to provide the last word on this technique, but hope to offer some ideas and examples that may be helpful.

Weave Structures for Warp-float and Weft-float Pleating

A variety of structures may create the pleated effect, and they can be used in different combinations to vary the texture of the cloth (*see* overleaf). Han damask needs the fewest shafts since each face can be woven on a minimum of three shafts, but there is an advantage in spreading it on to four shafts, so that four-shaft twills can be woven on the same warp.

Han damask has an interesting, slightly rough texture. Smoother-textured pleats result from using uneven twills and satins in the same way, and these can also be combined with Han damask to give pleats with a smooth surface on one face of the cloth and more textured pleats on the other.

Broken 3/1 twill avoids a twill line and approximates closely to a satin for these pleated structures. However, a true satin can be used in a similar way, though it will obviously require more shafts. Five-shaft satin can be combined with Han damask (on three shafts) so only eight shafts are needed, but because these weaves repeat on different numbers of picks (five and four), twenty picks are needed for a complete repeat. If sufficient shafts are available, uneven twills and satins with longer floats can also be used in the same way.

On a practical note, it is often assumed that such weaves will need floating selvedges or extra shafts for plain weave selvedges, but this is not essential. These structures make a perfectly acceptable selvedge, and in any case, the rolling of the fabric tends to conceal the edge.

Turning the Draft

This account of the structure assumes that the design consists of stripes running along the length of the warp. But of course, all the warp-float and weft-float structures that I have described can be turned so that the stripes run across the warp instead of along it. Only four shafts are then required, for twills or Han damask. I have found that this can work particularly well for weaving garments 'sideways' – so that the weft will run vertically in the finished garment – because the selvedges will then produce neat edges that do not need hemming. The following discussion of the factors involved assumes that the pleating runs along the length of the warp, but the general principles involved apply also to the turned structure.

Choice of Yarns

Although the ridged or pleated texture depends partly on the weave structure, the yarn and sett are also important, since the effect emerges from the interaction of structure and material. I have already mentioned the similarity with knitting, and this raises an interesting question about the extent to which relaxation of the *warp* floats, as well as the weft floats, contributes to the effect. Looking at the cross-sectional diagrams that were given earlier, it is easy to visualize the way that the relaxation of weft floats can pull in the fabric to create pleats – but what are the warp floats doing?

In the case of knitting, the lengthways loops on the knit side are inevitably of the same yarn as the crossways loops on the purl side of the fabric. In weaving, the warp and weft can be different yarns, allowing materials with different characteristics to be used. In fact, this is one of the easiest ways to achieve very pronounced pleating, for example by using a 'passive' warp and an 'active', shrinking yarn for the weft. It seems intuitively obvious that this arrangement will encourage pleating, as the weft floats shrink and cause fabric curling. However, this simple explanation is complicated by the awkward fact that successful pleating is often also produced with the same yarn for *both* warp and weft. In this case, if a yarn shrinks sufficiently weftways to give good pleating, then the warp floats must also be shrinking. Samples comparing yarns with different shrinkage do indeed suggest that such warp shrinkage may assist the formation of prominent pleats, although compared with the case of weft floats, it is less obvious why this should be so. However, it seems clear that each of the warp-float faces would curl up if it were free to do so, but as they are alternating, they try to curl in opposite directions. This natural tendency to pull away from one another probably assists the formation of pleats – once again, the analogy with knitting is helpful. In the case of weaving, there

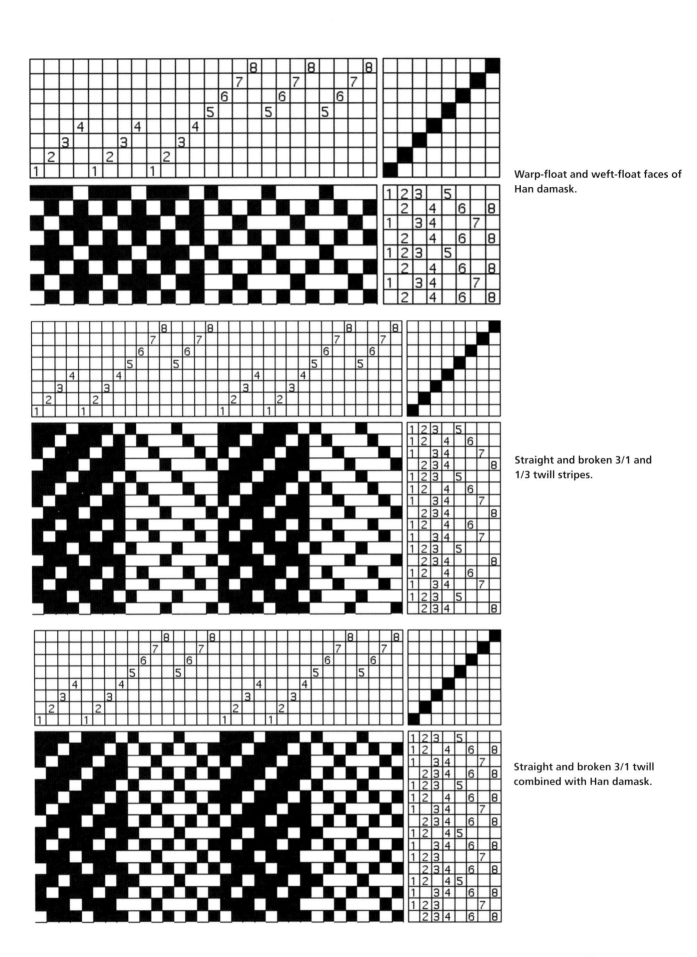

Warp-float and weft-float faces of Han damask.

Straight and broken 3/1 and 1/3 twill stripes.

Straight and broken 3/1 twill combined with Han damask.

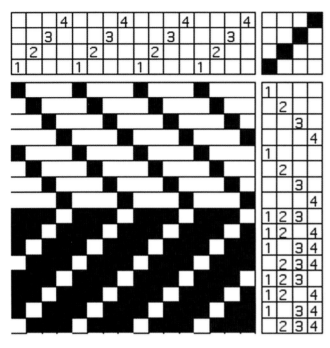

Weftways twill pleats.

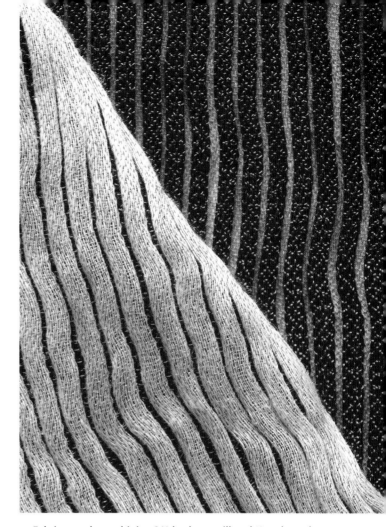

Fabric sample combining 3/1 broken twill and Han damask.

is an additional factor: the warp floats are running along the length of the fabric without interruption, while the weft is constantly forced from one face to the other. This arrangement tends to push the weft out of the fabric, forming longer floats that can more easily contract in the finishing. Other factors also have this effect (*see* below).

Shrinking Wefts

Clearly, a complex combination of factors is responsible for the ridged or pleated effect. However, given that yarn shrinkage does appear to be a major influence, it is certainly useful to find yarn that will show a reasonable amount of shrinkage when washed, particularly if it is to be used for weft. Yarn shrinkage can be due to the fibre or the yarn construction, or both. For example, tussah silk tends to shrink quite strongly, much more so than cultivated silk. Also, though yarns in all fibres show some shrinkage along their length when wetted out, due to fibre swelling, this is generally more noticeable in compact, firmly twisted yarns (even if these are balanced yarns) because there is less free space within them compared with more lightly twisted yarns.

Unbalanced yarns, in all fibres, shrink noticeably during finishing and may be suitable, but those that are only *slightly*

unbalanced are usually the most successful. Many so-called 'normal' yarns (even plied ones) are not perfectly balanced, and they can be tested for snarling twist (*see* Chapter 1) by taking a length of yarn and seeing whether it tends to ply back on itself. It may also be worth wetting out a small sample, in case a yarn has been set to make it stable for handling. Yarns that have been treated in this way may appear perfectly balanced while dry, but show a plying reaction when wetted.

Extremely highly twisted yarns do not always work so well, since their power may easily overwhelm the weave structure rather than cooperate with it. High-twist worsteds (such as industrial crepe wools) tend to spiral through the fabric at their own rhythm, creating a crepon effect that disrupts the stripes, rather than shaping them into pleats. However, this is mainly a problem when the crepe yarn is relatively similar in thickness to the warp. If crepe yarns are very much finer than the warp, they may work well, because their smaller-scale movements (relative to the warp thickness) are not likely to disturb the warp, and they shrink very strongly.

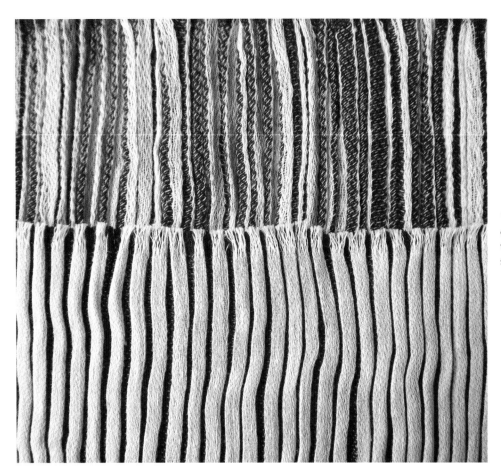

Top: Crepe wool spirals at its own rhythm. *Bottom*: Fine silk weft 'cooperates' with the weave structure to create regular pleats.

Pleating with Normal-twist Yarns

The arrangement described above, of normal yarns in the warp and unbalanced yarns in the weft, works very well for lightweight fabrics such as scarves. Pleating usually emerges naturally with relatively open setts (about 55–65 per cent as calculated by the Ashenhurst formula). However, if normal-twist yarns are to be used for both warp and weft, the effect is more unpredictable, and other influences often need to be brought into play. There seem to be two basic options: increasing the sett or using combinations of thin and thick yarns.

Increased Cloth Setting

Increasing the overall sett of the cloth often works well, particularly if using exactly the same yarn for warp and weft. This may be done through a moderate increase in the sett of both warp and weft (maintaining a balanced sett), or by considerably increasing either the warp sett or weft picking. Using a closer sett for the element that runs *across* the pleats (that is, a dense weft for lengthways pleats or a dense warp for crossways pleats) is often very effective in creating ridges or pleats but makes a rather firm fabric, so is better suited to furnishings or table linens than clothing fabrics. The Swedish firm Växbo Lin produces a ridged linen tablecloth with warp- and weft-float satin stripes running *across* the fabric (*see* Chapter 2), and this has the warp at almost twice the sett of the weft. In this design, 'Våga', the width of the stripes is also important, being relatively narrow (only five picks, giving one repeat of a five-end satin). This tends to produce the effect of a gently ridged texture, rather than a definite pleat, which is obviously well suited to table linen.

When working in this way, the required setts can really only be established by experiment, to suit the yarns involved, but at least 70 per cent of the maximum (Ashenhurst formula) is likely to be necessary. So a practical sampling approach is to start by setting the warp at roughly 70 per cent of its maximum, and then to experiment with different pickings. This method of creating pleats probably works by restricting the space within the fabric for yarn shrinkage, so that the forces generated cannot be dissipated within the structure, but instead begin to distort the fabric. As reasonably high setts are usually necessary, the fabrics are generally fairly firm and so are more suitable for garments and for household textiles than for scarves.

Thick/Stiff Warp and Fine Weft

An alternative approach, which works very well for lightweight fabrics, is to use a thicker or stiffer yarn for the warp than for the weft. Instead of the yarn crimp being distributed equally between warp and weft (warp and weft bending around one another), the finer, more flexible weft picks are forced to bend around the warp ends, so that the crimp is mainly in the weft. In effect, the weft picks are being pushed out of the fabric, forming longer floats that have more scope for shrinkage. To make the most of this effect, it is helpful during wet finishing to pull firmly lengthways on the fabric to achieve 'crimp interchange', transferring as much crimp as possible from warp to weft, to further encourage pleating.

The greater the difference in size between the warp and weft, the more readily pleating emerges. In the case of relatively soft, flexible yarns, the difference in size between warp and weft needs to be quite considerable. However, if the warp yarn is much *stiffer* than the weft, such as a linen warp with a silk weft, this also forces crimp into the weft, so the size difference between the two sets of yarns does not need to be so great.

The size relationship between different yarns can be expressed either in terms of yarn count/yardage, or yarn diameter. Although these work equally well, it is important not to confuse them. For example, a yarn of count 120/2 Nm obviously has twice the yardage of one that is 60/2 Nm, and so may be thought of as being half as 'thick', but this is in the sense of it having half the *volume* of the finer one, not half the *diameter*. The yarn diameter can be worked out from the yardage using the Ashenhurst formula, or estimated by 'wrapping' (*see* Chapter 3). Given that yarn diameters need to be known for cloth setting, it is useful to work these out for all the yarns you have in stock and to keep a record of them. If this has been done, then it is convenient to use yarn diameters as a quick method of comparing yarn thickness.

Alternatively, yarn counts can be used (provided that all the yarns are numbered on the same count system), or yardages can be compared.

With soft yarns, such as spun silk, some degree of pleating begins to emerge reliably when the diameter of the weft is about 70 per cent that of the warp, though it may be necessary to pull rather firmly lengthways to persuade the pleats to form. As the difference in size between warp and weft becomes greater, pleating develops increasingly easily, and it will emerge very strongly by the time the diameter of the weft is approximately half that of the warp. Alternatively, these relationships could be thought of in terms of yardages – the equivalent rule of thumb being that pleating will begin to emerge when the weft is twice the yardage of the warp, and will occur very easily by the time the weft is about four times the yardage of the warp. With stiff warp yarns, such as linen, pleats will tend to form more readily, so smaller differences between warp and weft will usually be successful.

Cloth Setting with Thick Warps and Fine Wefts

These pleated effects, emerging from the relationship of differently sized yarns, also depend on suitable setts. It is important to remember that there are two ways of thinking of the density of cloth setting: either as the number of ends and picks/cm (or inch), or in terms of the *percentage* of the maximum that would have been possible for that yarn, in that structure. In the case of a balanced sett, these two measures will only coincide when the warp and weft are the same size.

When producing lightweight fabrics, such as scarves, it is obviously desirable to avoid a very close sett that is likely to give a rather hard fabric. On the other hand, if the fabric is very loosely set, the forces involved can be dissipated through the open structure, causing the pleating to be weak and lacking in definition. Some experimentation may be needed to find a good, functional compromise, but it is generally successful to have a moderately open overall sett (55–65 per cent) but with a much higher percentage sett for the warp than the weft.

When combining thick warps with fine wefts, a relatively balanced sett, in terms of the *number of ends and picks*, often works particularly well. This creates a fabric in which the warp is dominant, as regards the *quantity* of material, giving a good drape to the cloth, but which also has stability because

WORKING OUT PERCENTAGE SETTS

You will find it is useful not only to keep a record of the warp and weft setts that prove successful, but also to work out percentages in relation to maximum sett. This information can then be used as a starting point for new designs using thicker or finer yarns. In this book, these percentage calculations are based on yarn diameters derived by the Ashenhurst formula, but you could use 'wrapped' estimates of diameter in the same way.

It is important to remember that a balanced sett will only give the same *percentage* setts for the two sets of yarns if the warp and weft are both of the same thickness. When working with warp-float/weft-float pleats, and using thick warp yarns with finer wefts, a balanced sett (in terms of epi and ppi) is often very successful, but this will give very different results in terms of the percentage setts of the yarns.

Example:

A warp-float/weft-float pleat fabric has been set at 56 epi and 56 ppi.

Warp: Spun silk 60/2. Yarn diameter = 112 diameters/inch
The maximum sett for a twill weave = $\frac{2}{3} \times 112 = 75$
The warp sett is 56 epi. $56/75 \times 100 = 75$ per cent

The warp sett is 75 per cent of the maximum.

Weft: Spun silk 210/2. Yarn diameter = 210 diameters/inch
The maximum sett for a twill weave = $\frac{2}{3} \times 210 = 140$
The weft sett is 56 ppi. $54/140 \times 100 = 40$ per cent

The weft sett is 40 per cent of the maximum.

The fabric has a balanced sett (epi and ppi), but in terms of the percentage setts, the warp is much more closely set.

there is a balance of *intersections* between warp and weft. So in terms of *percentage* sett, the warp is rather closely set, while the weft is relatively open. It is useful, when sampling, to work out and record percentage setts as well as ends and picks/inch (*see* box).

Turned Structure

The information given above concerning thick warps and fine wefts, assumes that the design consists of pleats running along the length of the warp. Remember that if the design is turned so that the pleats are running *across* the warp, then relaxation of the warp floats will be the most important factor, so pleating will be produced most easily if the warp is finer or less stiff than the weft. The relationship of warp and weft settings will also need to be turned so that the warp is more openly sett (in percentage terms) than the weft.

Width of Stripes

Whatever technique is used to create the pleating, the width of the stripes will also influence the effect. If the stripes are very narrow, the fabric has hardly had a chance to curl in one direction before it has to curl back the other way, and a faint ribbed effect will be produced rather than a distinct pleat. This can work very well for certain purposes, such as table linens, which need to avoid being too heavily textured, and as already mentioned, it has been used very effectively by the Swedish firm Växbo Lin to produce a finely ribbed tablecloth.

As stripes are made progressively wider, a distinct effect of gently rounded pleating begins to emerge. However, eventually a point will be reached where the stripes are so wide that they begin to flatten and sag, rather than producing a rounded pleat. Of course, such different effects are partly determined by the thickness and stiffness of the yarns. Heavier or stiffer yarns create pleats with more body, which can be wider than those woven from yarns that are more delicate. In general, at least eight ends will be required if a definite pleated effect is required, but for finer yarns, twelve or sixteen ends are usually necessary to produce a wide enough stripe. In terms of physical measurement, when working with reasonably fine, soft yarns, successful stripes for pleating seem typically to fall between 0.2 and 0.5in (0.5 and 1.27cm) in width, but much wider stripes can work well with stiffer or heavier yarns.

Alternate stripes are of linen, in broken twill, and a mix of tussah and silk noil, in Han damask (the linen and silk warps are run from separate beams). The silk yarns shrink more strongly than the linen, giving a rippled effect to the linen pleats.

Pleat Variations

One of the advantages of the pleating technique is that, though simple, it is open to many variations. It is easy, while warping, to vary the colours of the stripes across the warp or to use contrasting colours for the warp- and weft-float stripes, so that the fabric is double sided. Contrasting materials can also be used in alternate stripes to increase the textural variations. For example, if linen and silk are alternated, the silk will shrink more than the linen, giving a rippled texture to the pleats. Another method of causing the pleats to ripple is to use unbalanced yarns, with opposite twists in warp and weft. The typical undulating textures of Z × S interactions (*see* Chapter 4) will then develop in the fabric.

Reversing the Weave

If different colours have been used for the warp- and weft-float stripes, then reversing the weave structure will create a sharp change of colour across the warp, as the weft-float stripes become warp-float stripes, and vice versa. Repeated reversals will create a design of stripes running across the warp. To get a complete reversal of structure, you will need to weave a

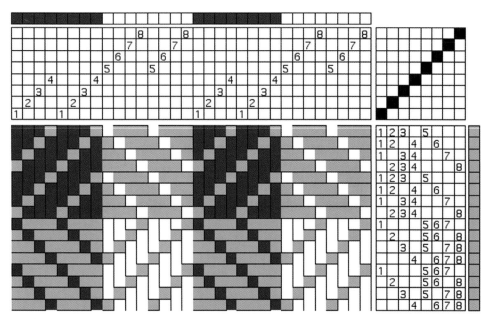

LEFT:
Reversing the structure will create stripes that run across the warp.

BOTTOM LEFT:
A weftways stripe is produced simply by reversing the structure. Warp: Linen/steel and spun silk. Weft: Spun silk.

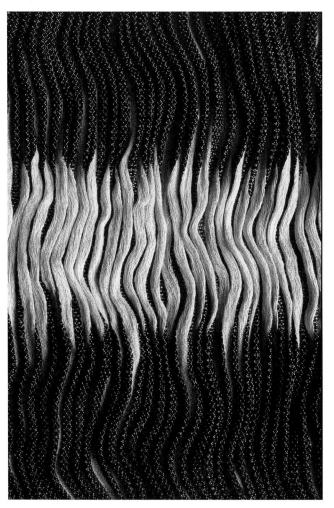

reasonable amount before reversing, and though this will vary depending on the weft yarn, at least 2in (5cm) will normally be necessary. Reversals that are more frequent than this will tend to cause the cloth to flatten out rather than forming reversed pleats. If the weft colour is kept the same throughout (as in the draft shown here), then some care needs to be taken while weaving because such reversals may be only faintly visible on the loom, especially if a very fine weft is being used. In this case, the stripe that is formed by the reversal is purely structural, and only emerges when the fabric is wet finished. You could also create more dramatic colour effects by using contrasting colours in the weft to coincide with the structure reversals. A further possibility, if enough shafts are available, is to set up the loom to allow isolated blocks of reversed structure to be woven. If the design is turned, so the pleating runs across the warp, then only eight shafts will be needed to get this effect. Andreas Möller weaves 'sideways' in this way, using a very wide loom, to produce boldly patterned pleated scarves and throws (*see* his website for examples).

Making Deeper Pleats

As already mentioned, there is a limit to how large the pleats can be before they begin to sag and flatten. However, it is possible to create deeper pleats by inserting stripes of a flat weave (such as plain, twill) in between the warp- and weft-float stripes. In this case, extra shafts are required so that a deep pleated structure will need ten or twelve shafts, assuming that the pleat stripes have been produced with 1/3 and 3/1 twills. However, there are some other constructions that will create deep pleats within the limit of eight shafts. One possibility is to use three-shaft structures for the warp-float/weft-float stripes, such as Han damask or three-shaft twills. This will free up two shafts to be used for plain weave.

An alternative is to use 1/3 and 3/1 twills for the pleating and to produce the 'flat' stripes using the *same* shafts, but with a rearranged threading, to give frequent reversals of the warp- and weft-float faces, such as two ends of each. This creates areas of faintly ridged, but otherwise flat fabric (refer to the chapter 'Tricot Weaves' in Oelsner's *A Handbook of Weaves* – *see* Bibliography). It is interesting to note that a comparable strategy can be used in knitting to make deep pleating, where a section of flat ribbing (one plain, one purl) is followed by several knit stitches, which cause the fabric to bend. This is followed by another section of flat ribbing and, finally, several purl stitches, causing the fabric to bend back the other way.

Sampling for Pleating

You may be thinking that it is surprising that really satisfactory pleating can be produced at all, given that there are so many demands to be satisfied, in terms of yarns, stripe widths and setts, while also attending to the handle and drape of the fabric! It is true that steering a middle course between the various requirements may sometimes take a bit of care, but this is precisely why sampling is so important. The flexibility of the technique also makes sampling particularly worthwhile, as so many different cloth qualities and effects can be produced. A willingness to sample extensively, reflect on the results and keep careful records of your experiments is vital to successful designing. Sampling will be discussed in more detail in Chapter 10, making particular reference to warp-float/weft-float pleating, which will be used as a 'case study' of the process of building on experience.

Cord Weaves

Cord weaves are a group of structures with relatively long floats, running in ordered lines along the back of the fabric. These floats shrink during finishing to create a ridged effect on

the face. The following drafts show the face of the weave, but in practice it may sometimes be more convenient to weave these fabrics upside down, particularly if working on a table loom, since fewer shafts then need to be lifted. The simplest cords can be woven on four shafts. Cords can be woven with either alternating or paired picks, and if the weft is the same throughout, these are equally easy to weave. However, if two shuttles are used, for example to insert different colours or qualities of yarn, then it is slightly quicker to throw pairs of picks than alternating ones, and the cloth quality is similar.

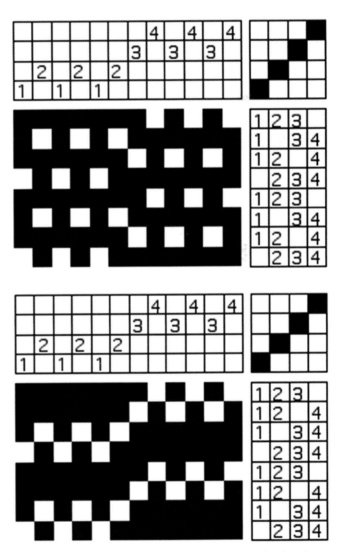

Four-shaft cord weaves, with alternating picks (top) and paired picks (bottom).

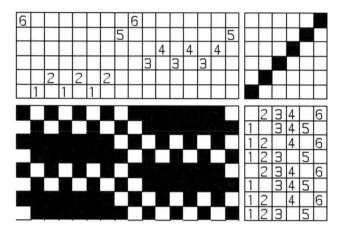

Bedford cord with cutting line.

Although it is useful to be able to produce a cord on only four shafts, it is more usual to emphasize the ridges by using two extra shafts to create a 'cutting line' between them, giving a classic weave structure, namely Bedford cord. Even normal-twist yarns will create texture with these cord structures, but particularly well defined ridges can be created with high-twist wefts.

Additional shafts can also be used to introduce wadding ends, and an even bolder texture will then be produced. Such wadding ends need to be raised and lowered in a sequence that causes them to remain between the face of the cloth and the floats. As they do not weave into the fabric, these ends take up differently and must be tensioned separately from the rest of the warp. There are many different ways in which cords can be varied. For example, twills or other weave structures could be used for the face of the cord instead of plain weave, and there is also plenty of scope for colour variations in both warp and weft. Sharon Alderman in her book *Mastering Weave Structures* (*see* Bibliography) explores the possibilities very thoroughly.

These prominent cords are produced using a normal-twist weft for the cord itself (woven in Han damask) while a high-twist weft floats on the back of the fabric. The bold texture is further emphasized by wadding the cords and using stripes of a backed twill between them.

Cords with Separate Weaving and Floating Picks

Although a high-twist weft will shrink to produce very *promi-nent* cords, it will also tend to disturb the *surface* of the cords themselves, giving them a crinkly texture. To create cords that are prominent but also have a smooth surface, it is necessary to structure the cord so that there are different 'weaving' and 'floating' picks. A high-twist yarn need only then be used for the floating picks, while a normal-twist yarn forms the face of the fabric.

Combining Cords with Plain Weave

It can also be interesting to combine the cords with larger stripes of another weave, such as plain weave, to create a tex-ture of sharp ridges against a flat background. If there are to be relatively large areas of plain weave, it will be more conve-nient to adjust the threading to put these ends on the front shafts, and move back the cord ends.

When weaving with two shuttles, it is convenient to use a cord structure with paired picks. However, a construction that relies on alternating picks is worth using in some cas-es. A firmer fabric can be produced if each pick of normal yarn is followed by a floating pick of high-twist yarn that lies in the *same* shed for the flat sections of the fabrics. These

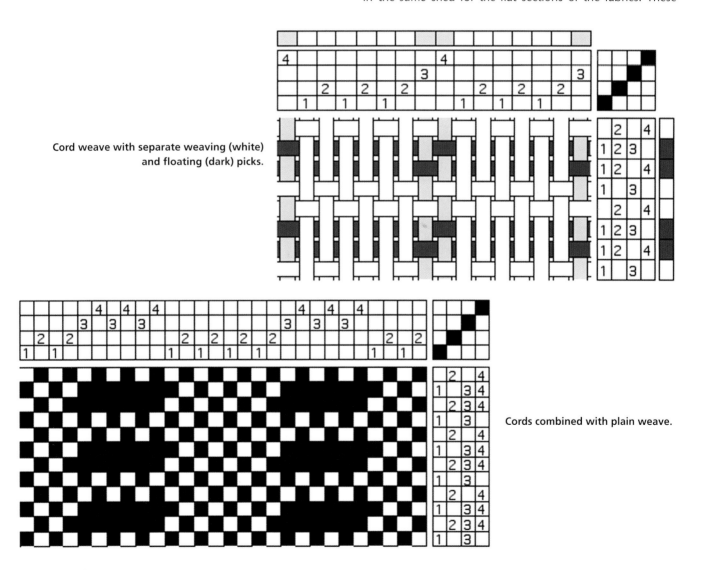

Cord weave with separate weaving (white) and floating (dark) picks.

Cords combined with plain weave.

85

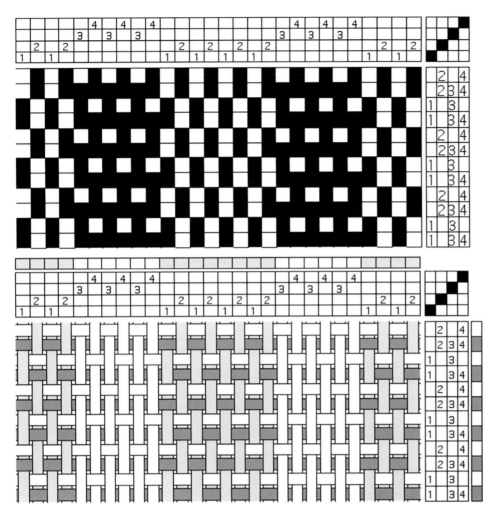

Cords combined with half hopsack. Each plain weave pick is followed by a floating pick that lies in the same shed for the flat areas of the fabric, only floating in the cord areas. The white ends can be seen forming the cord, while the grey ends weave half hopsack. The white picks (normal yarn) weave to form the face of the fabric. The grey picks (high-twist yarn) float behind the cords but weave into the fabric for the half hopsack stripes.

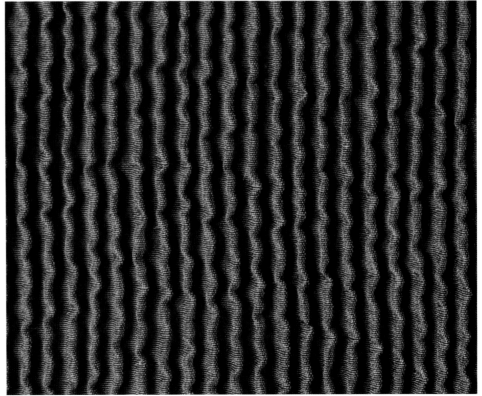

This industrially produced silk fabric combines normal and crepe yarns, in a structure of cords and half hopsack. As the cord ends have fewer interlacements, they form a more open fabric than the half hopsack, creating an effect of softly rippling cords on a firmer ground. (Designer unknown)

consequently form a half hopsack structure rather than plain weave. This structure is shown both as a weave draft and as a thread diagram to make the structure clearer.

Using Cord Weaves to Make Pleats

Traditionally the cord surface forms the face of the cloth, while the weft floats are confined to the back. However, if the warp-float and weft-float faces of the cords are alternated across the width of the fabric, ridges will form on both sides of the cloth. It is then possible to create sharp-edged pleats of various widths, if stripes of a 'flat' weave structure, such as plain weave, are inserted between relatively narrow alternating cords. Effectively, the cords are simply being used to encourage the fabric to bend at these points. The general principle is very similar to that described for warp-float/weft-float deep pleating in the previous section, but cords tend to give a sharper edge to the pleats.

There is an advantage in using the cord structure with separate 'weaving' and 'floating' picks: a fairly crisp, normal-twist yarn can then be used for the 'weaving' picks, while a high-twist yarn is used for the 'floating' picks. This helps to create a smooth texture for the faces of the pleats and makes the cords more distinct. The structure needs a minimum of six shafts, but if eight are available, it is best to spread the plain weave over four shafts, especially when working with fine yarns. If more shafts are available, other structures could, of course, be used for either the flat stripes or the cords.

There are endless possibilities with such pleated structures, since the width of the flat stripes, or the sequence of the warp- and weft-float cords, can be varied to create different types of pleating – accordion pleats, knife pleats, box pleats, and so on. If different colours are used for the cords and the pleats and/or the different faces of the pleats, this will emphasize the pleated structure, and various arrangements can be used to conceal or reveal the colours in different ways. Paper folding is a quick way of experimenting with such effects before investing time in sampling. Paul Jackson in *Folding Techniques for Designers: From Sheet to Form* (*see* Bibliography) gives a detailed account of how paper folding can be used to create many different styles of pleating.

Many different fabric qualities are also possible, depending on the materials used, but the fabric does need to be firm enough to maintain the form of the pleat, especially in the case of accordion pleats. A fairly stiff weft yarn, such as medium weight linen, is helpful for the 'weaving' picks, to give a crisp texture to the fabric. If a lightweight fabric is required, then finer and softer yarns may still be successful if additional picks of a stiffer yarn are included at intervals, since these can act as 'struts' and give body to the pleats. The structure of insect wings is instructive in this respect (*see* Chapter 10).

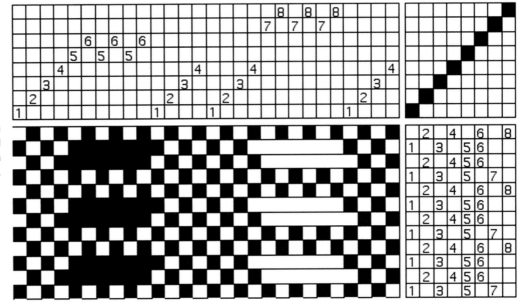

Plain weave combined with alternating warp-float and weft-float cords, to create a pleated effect.

'Dragonfly Pleat' scarf. A linen warp is crossed by wefts of very fine hard silk and crepe silk. This creates a delicate, translucent pleated effect, but periodic picks of a stiffer linen yarn are needed to give body to the pleats.

'Silk Pleat' scarf. Warp: Spun silk. Weft: Hard silk and crepe silk, with additional picks of linen.

'Steel Pleat', an experimental piece, combining structural pleats with the 'memory' given to the fabric by a silk/steel warp yarn.

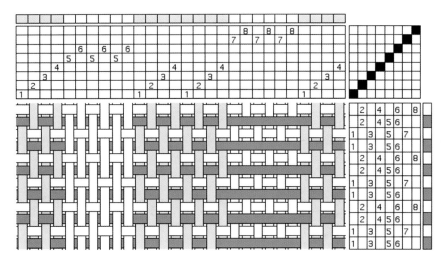

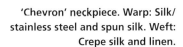

Alternating cords combined with half hopsack. The white weft indicates a normal yarn, while the high-twist weft is shown in grey.

'Chevron' neckpiece. Warp: Silk/stainless steel and spun silk. Weft: Crepe silk and linen.

'Möbius' neckpiece. Warp: Silk/stainless steel and spun silk. Weft: Crepe silk and linen.

Striking effects are also possible through including more unconventional yarns, especially those in which traditional textile fibres are combined with metal. Silk twisted together with stainless steel makes a particularly intriguing yarn; when this is used as warp, it gives a fabric with interesting mixed properties. Permanent 'natural' pleats can be produced in the normal way, but the silk/steel yarn gives extra stiffness to the fabric, together with a temporary 'memory' for additional pleats and distortions. So the combined effect of a traditional crepe yarn and a 'high-tech' yarn produces fabric properties that neither could achieve alone.

The unusual fabric qualities produced by such a traditional/high-tech combination are ideal for making textile jewellery, which is lightweight, flexible, washable and comfortable to wear. A weave structure in which the cords are combined with half hopsack, rather than plain weave, works particularly well in this case, especially if stiff yarns such as linen or paper are used as the 'weaving' picks (*see* draft). This gives a firm texture that helps to maintain the form of the pleats when weaving these small-scale jewellery pieces.

The neckpieces shown opposite are woven as single layers of cloth and then sewn to form tubular pieces. They could, in principle, be woven as tubes, but in practice it seems quicker and easier to weave a single layer. This also leaves open the option of creating Möbius pieces or inserting multiple twists before joining the edges. The pieces shown here are designed to be simply pulled over the head, relying on the elasticity given by the natural pleating. With repeated wear they do tend to stretch, but if a piece becomes too loose it can simply be soaked in water to re-establish the natural pleats. However, it would also be possible to design a fastening rather than joining the edges, and this would help to prevent the pieces from stretching so easily.

Weftways Cords or Piqués

Any of these weaves can be turned to give a corded or pleated effect running across the warp. A weftways equivalent of the classic Bedford cord (where all ends will be weaving in and floating by the same amount) will need only one warp beam. However, just as when working with warpways cords, there is often an advantage in separating the threads into 'weavers' and 'floaters' to make the best use of the different properties of high-twist and normal yarns. These will tend to take up differently and so may need to be separately tensioned.

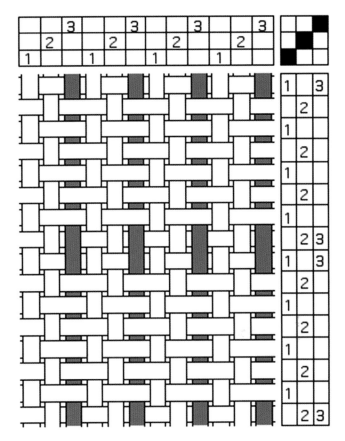

Piqué or Welt. The floating ends are set at a higher tension than the face ends and stitch into the face cloth to create a texture. If a high-twist yarn is used for the floating ends, this will further increase the texture.

However, because of the forgiving nature of high-twist yarns, it is sometimes possible to manage with one beam, at least for fairly short warps.

If two beams are available, then it is possible to use two warps run at very different tensions, giving a classic weave structure: piqué. While the woven face of the cloth is lightly tensioned, a higher tension is put on the floating warp, which creates a strong texture as it stitches into the face weave. This structure is usually woven with two face cloth ends to one stitching end, and using normal yarns for both warps, giving a firm quality to the fabric. However, if the stitching warp is made with high-twist yarns, this will further emphasize the texture and give a fabric that is springy in the warp direction. The simplest piqué, with straight ridges running across the

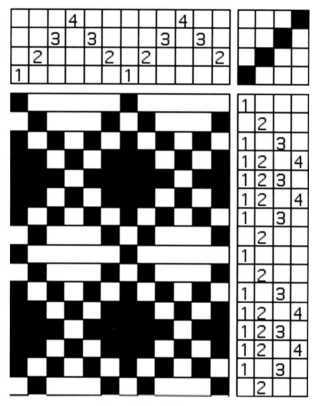

Four-shaft waffle weave.

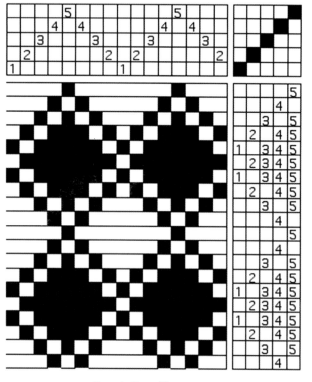

Five-shaft waffle weave.

cloth, is also known as a welt. The stitching points can be arranged to give more complex designs, such as waved effects (refer to Sharon Alderman's *Mastering Weave Structures* – *see* Bibliography – for more on piqués).

Clearly there are many possibilities for varying these cord and piqué structures, so it makes sense to be flexible and not always to stick rigidly to standard 'textbook' weaves. For example, a range of structures could be designed, running either warpways or weftways, using different ratios of plain weave ends to floating ends, depending on the stiffness of the normal yarn and the power of the high-twist yarn.

Other Float Structures

Two groups of weaves have just been described that rely on very regular rows of floats to create ridged or pleated effects, but there are also many traditional structures that have floats distributed over the entire surface of the fabric. Some of these are designed to create a highly organized texture, while others aim for a more random effect.

Waffle (Honeycomb) Weaves

Waffle weaves are a useful way to use relatively few shafts to create long floats, which contract strongly when high-twist yarns are used. The smallest waffle weave can be produced on only four shafts using a point draft, but its floats are not really long enough to create a strong texture, and it is better to use more shafts if possible.

It is important to note that waffle weaves, like many other traditional float weaves, give very good textures even with normal, balanced or low-twist yarns. Simply substituting high-twist yarns may not always yield particularly striking *visual* results, though a useful increase in elasticity will certainly be produced. The problem is that if high-twist yarns are used throughout such a fabric, then *everything* shrinks, and this may have the effect of reducing the size of the fabric, while giving a rather similar textural appearance to that obtained with normal yarns. As one of my students recorded in her notebook, 'If you use high-twist yarns, then the sample gets smaller'!

One way round this is to open up the sett to such an extent that the crinkling of the high-twist yarns definitely becomes

Samples of seersucker fabric, using narrow bands of waffle weave to create the texture. Warp: Spun silk. Weft: Spun silk and high-twist wool.

a feature in itself (an excellent example of this can be seen in *Fuwa Fuwa* – one of the Nuno series of books). Another approach is to introduce some contrast, either of material, yarn twist or weave structure, so that shrinking and non-shrinking areas of fabric can be played off against one another. The point drafts that are normally used for waffle weaves make it easy to combine these structures with plain weave for contrast. However, it can sometimes be worthwhile spreading the structure on to more shafts, especially when sampling; for example, a five-shaft waffle weave could be set up with an eight-shaft straight draft, to allow a greater variety of other structures to be woven on the same warp.

One limitation of the simple waffle weaves is that these structures can give a rather regimented look. If more shafts are available, a very attractive and more varied effect can be produced with Brighton honeycomb. The smallest version of this structure could be woven on a straight draft with eight shafts (refer to Sharon Alderman's *Mastering Weave Structures* – *see* Bibliography – for a thorough account of waffle and Brighton honeycomb structures).

LEFT:
Fabric by Anna Champeney (Spain), in which waffle weave is combined with blocks of plain weave, to create contrasting areas of flat and crinkled cloth. (Photo: Anna Champeney)

BELOW:
This sculptural piece by Fiona Crestani uses strong contrasts of both structure and material. Waffle weave, woven with a crepe yarn, is combined with plain weave in rusting iron wire. (Photo: Fiona Crestani)

Alternating Float Weaves

The principle of building up weaves with floats on alternate ends and picks has traditionally been used to give textural and lace-like effects (for example huckaback, mock leno). Like waffle weaves, these structures have great potential for use with high-twist yarns as they can produce long floats on relatively few shafts and can easily be combined with plain weave for contrast. They have a further advantage in that, however long the float, each unit needs only two shafts. Consequently there is plenty of scope for using traditional block threading arrangements to contrast shrinking areas, consisting of spot or lace units, with more firmly woven areas of plain weave. Sharon Alderman (*Mastering Weave Structures*) and Madelyn van der Hoogt (*The Complete Book of Drafting for Handweavers – see* Bibliography) give excellent accounts of the drafting of these traditional weaves.

The standard mock leno weave has units with both warp and weft floats. An even more economical arrangement is given by a structure where all the float units are identical, separated by plain weave ends and picks, giving a cloth with weft floats on one face and warp floats on the other. The structure is the basis for Swedish and Bronson laces.

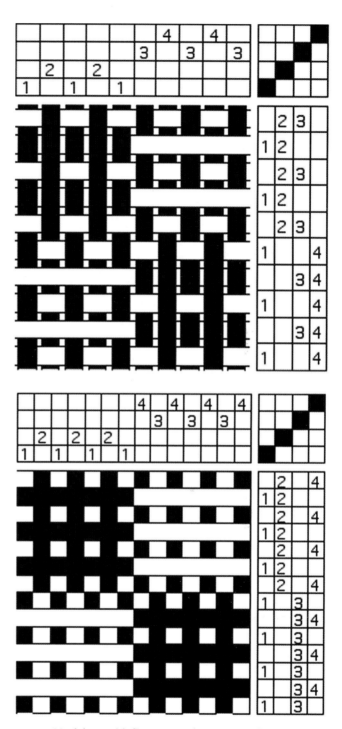

Mock leno with five-span and seven-span floats.

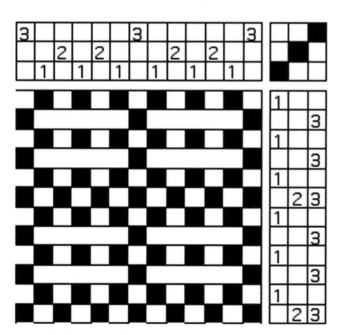

Weft-float face of the 'Swedish lace' type of mock leno.

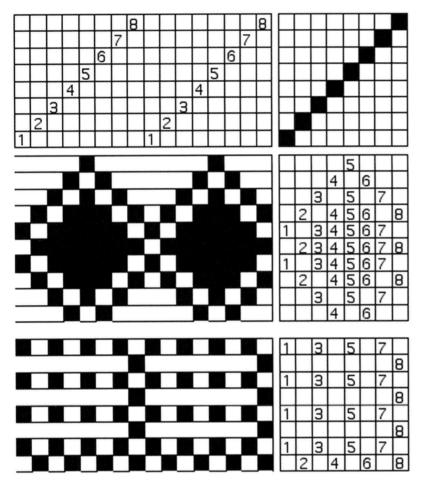

With a warp threaded on eight shafts, both Swedish lace and waffle weave could be sampled for seersucker effects, with these float weaves played off against plain weave.

Although these weaves can give a similar amount of contraction to the waffle weaves, they provide an interestingly different effect, retaining something of their lace-like character even when the yarns have contracted. It is often worth spreading them on to more than the minimum number of shafts, particularly when sampling, to allow different structures to be tried out on the same warp. For example, Swedish lace, with a seven-span float, can be threaded on eight shafts, so that waffle weave could be woven on the same warp, allowing the different fabric qualities to be compared.

Crepe Weaves

Although the 'classic' crepe of antiquity depends only on yarn twist in plain weave, more complex weaves have been developed which attempt to simulate the crepe effect with normal yarns. These use relatively short floats, in both warp and weft, distributed so as to create a rough irregular surface. Visually they do create an effect reminiscent of crepe texture, though less random, since there is always some tendency for patterning to emerge. Also, they do not produce the elasticity of 'real' crepe. Though they are usually made with normal, balanced yarns as a substitute for crepe, they could also be woven with high-twist yarns to emphasize the texture and give a more elastic effect. A good account of crepe weaves is given by Sharon Alderman (2004).

Plain Weave/Float Combinations

Strong textures can be produced by combining long floats with areas of closely woven plain weave, so that some areas of the cloth can easily shrink while others cannot. The most extreme textures will be obtained with structures that keep the 'floating' and 'weaving' threads separate. The closely

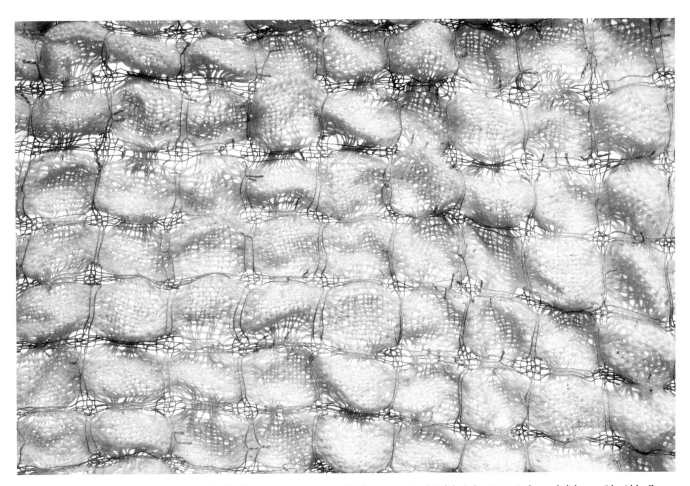

Blocks of plain weave are combined with floats to create a bubbled texture, in this fabric by Lotte Dalgaard. (Photo: Ole Akhøj)

woven areas can then be woven with passive yarns, while active yarns are used for the floats, so that the characteristics of the yarns and the structures reinforce one another. Contrasts of material can also be used in the same way, even with normal-twist yarns, for example, by playing off closely woven areas of linen against floats of wool. Many different arrangements of this basic idea are possible, and will create bubbled textures of various kinds.

There is a particularly interesting group of traditional structures with two sets of yarns, in both warp and weft, which differ in colour. Each colour of yarn interlaces only with itself, floating over or under the other set in the rest of the fabric. In standard industrial textbooks, such as Watson's *Textile Design and Colour*, these structures are categorized as a special type of colour-and-weave effect. Handweavers have recently started to refer to them as 'deflected double weaves', because many of them (though not all) give the superficial impression

of a double cloth. They are also sometimes called 'integrated cell weaves'. As well as their traditional use for colour effects, these structures offer considerable scope for texture, since the two sets of yarns can vary in terms of material or yarn twist as well as, or instead of, varying in colour, and the long floats allow for good shrinkage (refer to Vicki Masterson's article in *Fabrics That Go Bump* – *see* Bibliography).

Although some of these structures can give an impressive illusion of being double cloths (to the point where they are categorized by some weavers as 'false double weaves'), further possibilities for working with high-twist yarns and contrasts of material are offered by compound weaves, which really are constructed with two sets of elements in one or both directions. This may involve the doubling-up of either the warp or weft in 'backed' weaves, or both sets of yarns in true double cloths. These weaves will be considered in the next chapter.

CHAPTER 6

SUBTLE INTERPLAY: DOUBLING UP

All the structures described in the last chapter had only one warp and one weft. Although in some cases there were sets of yarns that were behaving in different ways, this still resulted in only a single layer of cloth. This chapter is concerned with compound structures that are truly double, and which offer additional design opportunities when working with high-twist yarns and contrasts of fibre.

'Cracking Up', a wool/silk double cloth that relies on the contrast between normal and high-twist yarns to create texture.

Double-Faced Weaves

These structures are sometimes known as 'backed' weaves, a term deriving from the practice of adding weight or strength to a fabric by using a cheaper yarn as a backing to a better quality yarn, in either the warp or weft direction. But the same structures can also be used to give different colours, patterns or textures to the two sides, with yarns of equal quality.

The simplest double-faced weave is constructed using two complementary sets of three-span floats. This structure has a long history as a patterning technique, and may be used warpways (warp-faced compound tabby) or weftways (weft-faced compound tabby, or taqueté). In either case, the

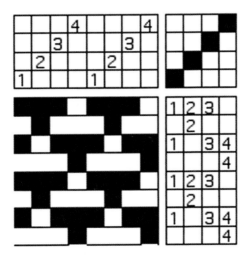
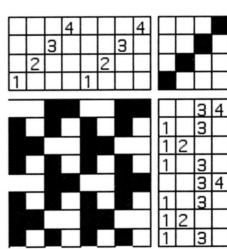

Left: Weft-faced compound tabby.
Right: Warp-faced compound tabby.

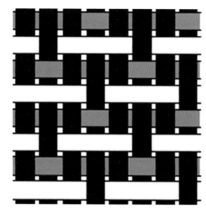
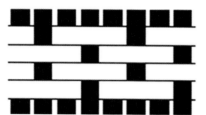
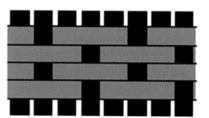

Left: Weft-faced compound tabby woven with two different coloured wefts. *Centre and right*: The visual effect of the two faces of the cloth when the weft is beaten down.

'Crepon Spot' scarf. This has a warp of alternate ends of black and white. The plain weave ground is patterned with spots of warp-faced compound tabby, which pushes the white ends to one face of the cloth and the black ends to the other. As in the case of the weft-faced structure shown above, the floats of one yarn conceal the intersections of the other. Warp: Spun silk. Weft: Crepe silk.

principle is that successive ends or picks float on the face and the reverse of the fabric in such a way that *the floats of one yarn conceal the intersections of the other*. If different colours are used, two strongly contrasting faces are produced, particularly if the element that is doubled is also closely set.

A weft-faced compound tabby requires only three shafts but can be spread on to four for flexibility in combining it with other structures. The equivalent structure warpways requires four shafts.

Double-faced weaves can be used in various ways to add pattern to crepe or crepon fabrics, and can either be introduced as an additional warp or weft, or can simply emerge from structural variations within a single warp, for example being combined with plain weave. These weaves could also be used to create texture in themselves, by using high-twist yarns for one face and normal yarns for the other, combined with stripe or block arrangements that reverse the faces.

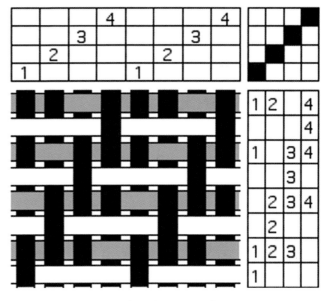

Weft-backed 1/3 twill.

Double-Faced Twills

Structures constructed on a similar principle can be based on twills or satins, and these tend to give better coverage and contrast between the faces. The simplest structure is based on 1/2 twill, but 1/3 twill is more commonly used. Once again, it is important to position the interlacing points so that they will be concealed between the floats of the other weft. The structure can be turned to give a warpways double-faced twill, but will then require eight shafts. As with the compound tabby weaves, double-faced twills can either be intrinsic to the cloth as a whole, or can be used as supplementary warps or wefts, in combination with other structures.

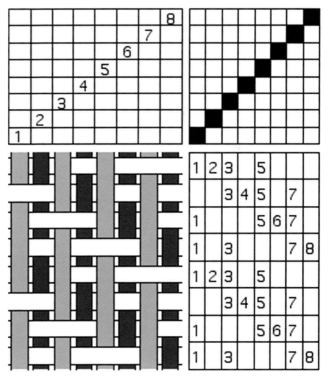

Warp-backed 3/1 twill.

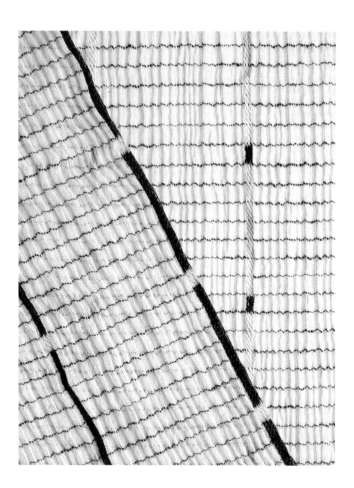

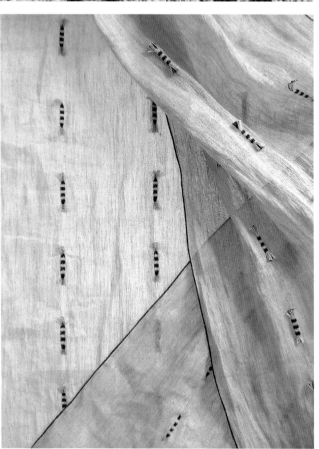

TOP LEFT:
In this scarf by Deirdre Wood (UK), a warp-backed twill is used to create pattern, but this is combined with cramming and spacing and a high-twist weft, to create a textured surface.

TOP RIGHT:
'Spot-stripe' scarf. An openly set, plain weave crepon fabric is patterned with dense stripes of warp-backed twill, to create a spot design. Warp: Linen. Weft: Crepe silk.

LEFT:
'Beelines' scarf. A plain weave crepe fabric is patterned with intermittent spots of warp-backed twill. Between the spots, the yarn floats – the surplus yarn is clipped away after the fabric has been washed. Warp: Linen and tussah silk. Weft: Crepe silk, Z and S yarns together on one pirn.

'Levende Striber' (Living Stripes). In this wool double cloth, Berthe Forchhammer (Denmark) creates a lively, delicate texture by using Z and S spun crepe yarns in both warp and weft. (Photo: Ole Akhøj)

Double Cloths

Working with double or multilayer cloths is such a huge area of design that a brief survey can do no more than give a flavour of the possibilities. Classic techniques, such as interchanging double cloth, work extremely well with high-twist yarns, but there are also many interesting ways of combining double cloth with single cloths of various structures.

Interchanging Double Cloth with High-Twist Yarns

If interchanging double plain cloths are used for patterning the fabric, then varied textures such as tracking, undulations, bouclé, crepon or crepe can be produced in the two layers, as described for single-layer cloths in Chapter 4. This can create very attractive fabrics with stripe or block designs, in which variations in colour are combined with the textures provided by the high-twist yarns.

If plenty of shafts are available, then more intricate designs can also work well with these textured surfaces. Many of Junichi Arai's beautiful fabrics rely on complex patterning by computer-controlled Jacquard looms, combined with lively textures created with high-twist yarns. Arai is also very adventurous in his use of different arrangements of layers: cloths may be double or quadruple, or may even be woven as double and be transformed into a single layer once they are off the loom.

A double-cloth scarf design by Reiko Sudo, which uses weft yarns of different twist to vary the crepon texture of the fabric. The main body of the scarf uses a high-twist yarn that forms a very fine, tight crepon, while a less highly twisted yarn is used for the border to create a gentler crepon effect. (Ann Sutton Collection)

This cotton double cloth by Junichi Arai has alternations of twist in both warp and weft, in both layers, creating a fine crepe texture that is springy in both directions. (Ann Sutton Collection)

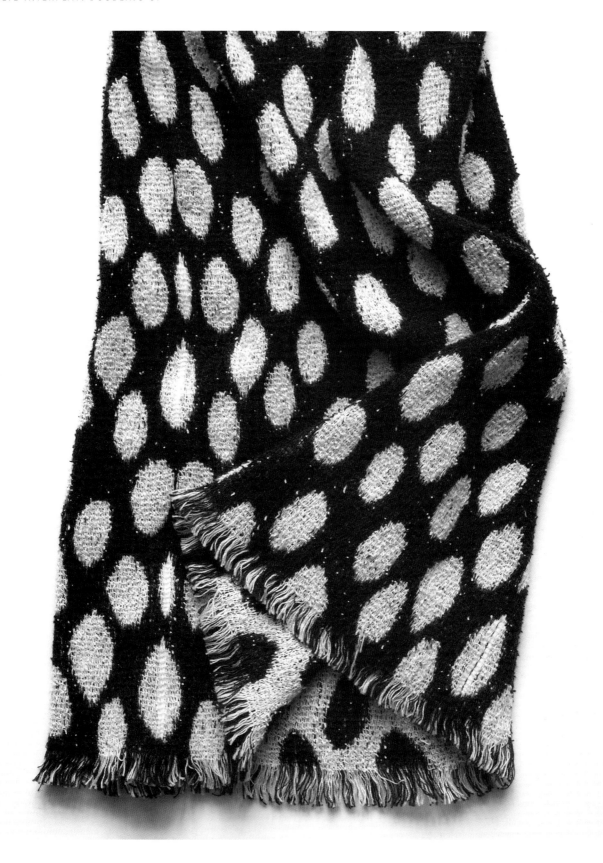

OPPOSITE:
This spotted fabric by Junichi Arai, with a normal cotton warp and high-twist cotton weft, is actually a four-layered cloth, since it forms a tube as well as using interchanging double cloth to create the pattern. The very open sett results in a bouclé effect as small twists of yarn protrude from the surface of the fabric. These twists effectively 'store' surplus yarn, so that the fabric is intensely stretchy.

RIGHT:
'Barkcloth' fabric by Junichi Arai. Like the spotted fabric shown opposite, this double cloth uses a normal cotton warp combined with a high-twist cotton weft, but the much closer sett results in a crepon texture.

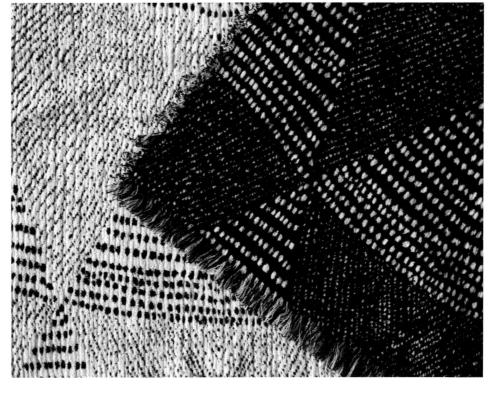

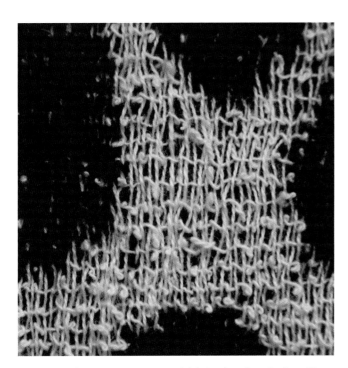

Detail of Junichi Arai's spotted fabric, showing the bouclé texture created by small twists of yarn escaping from the surface of the fabric.

Detail of 'Barkcloth', showing the crepon texture.

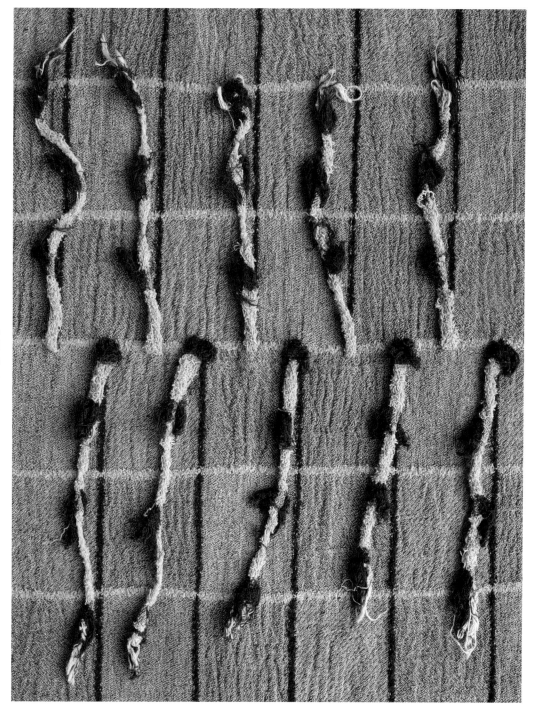

The fabric shown with the fringe laid out to reveal the original position of the yarns before cutting.

OPPOSITE:
A double cloth that becomes a single cloth. This ingenious fabric by Junichi Arai is woven as a double cloth, with some yarns floating in both warp and weft, before interweaving with each other and with the lower layer of fabric. The floats are later cut apart to create a fringe that emerges from various points in the fabric (see above). (Ann Sutton Collection)

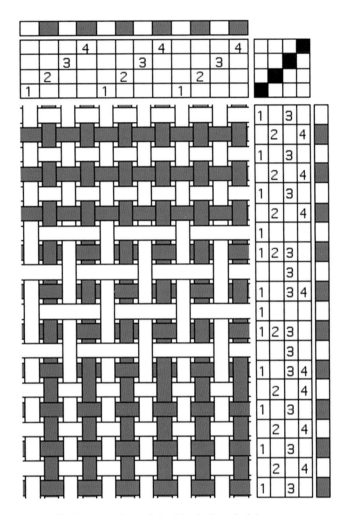

Weftways stripes of double cloth and plain weave.

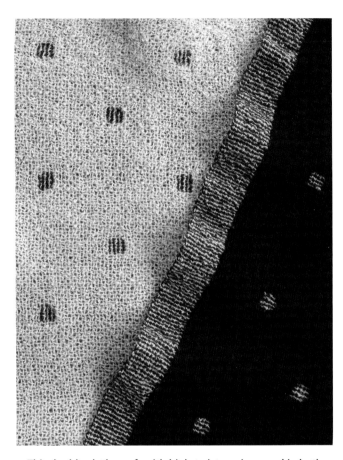

This double-cloth scarf, with high-twist merino wool in both warp and weft, is patterned with spots of single cloth, where the two layers weave together. The selvedge is also a single layer of cloth, and since it cannot shrink as much as the double cloth, this gives a gentle ripple to the edge of the scarf.

Combining Double and Single Structures

The combination of a double cloth with a single cloth provides another interesting way to create pattern. However, it can also be used to produce texture, by exploiting contrasts of shrinkage between an open double-cloth structure and a more closely set single cloth. For example, even on only four shafts, simple weftways stripes of double cloth and plain weave can create a seersucker effect, because the double weave is able to contract more readily than the plain weave. Of course, varying the yarn twist or materials used for the two types of cloth could create an even stronger texture. Colour contrasts also work well, giving small-scale colour-and-weave stripes in the plain weave that can play off against solid colours in the double weave.

If more shafts are available, there are infinite possibilities for both pattern and texture. Various arrangements of blocks, spots or stripes of double and single structures can provide the patterning for cloths whose surface is textured by high-twist yarns, or these patterns can themselves become the driving force behind the creation of texture, through variations in shrinkage from one area of the cloth to another.

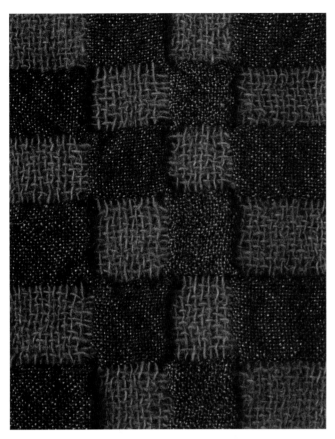

A non-shrinking layer (wool/silk) and a shrinking layer (high-twist woollen merino) interchange with one another. The shrinkage of the wool pushes the wool/silk cloth into relief. The fabric is the same on both sides. Warp and weft: Wool/silk and high-twist woollen merino.

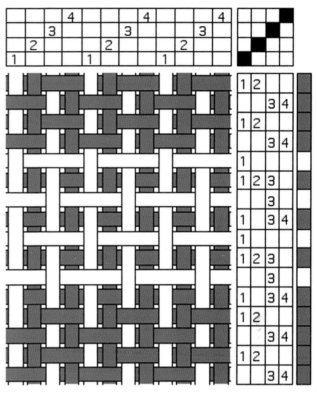

Double plain weave with half hopsack. The structure could be woven with high-twist yarn for the threads shown in grey and normal yarn for the white threads. Warpways shrinkage of the high-twist yarn would then throw the strips of white cloth into relief, and weftways shrinkage would impart a rippled effect.

Differential Shrinkage between Layers

In the double-cloth examples given so far, similar textures have been produced in both layers of cloth. Effectively, texture and pattern are complementing one another. But pattern blocks can also be a way of creating strong textures directly, if yarns with different shrinkage potential are used for the different layers of double or multilayer cloths. In order to produce texture in this way the layers will need to be *braced* against one another at certain points, so that when one shrinks the other is thrown into relief. There are various options: the cloths may simply interchange with one another (as in the fabric shown above left), or they can be joined together by stitching points

(where an end from one cloth interlaces with a pick of the other). A combination of double and single cloth (as described earlier) also works extremely well in bracing non-shrinking and shrinking areas of fabric against one another. However, in this situation plain weave may sometimes create a rather firm structure for the single cloth and, since this can limit the overall shrinkage of the fabric, it may impair the texture. Weaves with fewer intersections, such as half hopsack(shown in the draft above right) or twill, could instead be used for the single cloth to ensure that the fabric as a whole is sufficiently open and flexible to allow texture to develop.

'Cracking Up', a double cloth in which a layer of wool/silk and a layer of high-twist merino create texture through differential shrinkage. In certain areas, the separate layers weave together to form a single cloth, creating a grid pattern that braces the two cloths against one another. When the lower layer of red wool shrinks, the dark wool/silk surface is thrown into a texture. Some gaps have been left in the merino layer to create floats that increase shrinkage. Warp and weft: Wool/silk and high-twist woollen merino.

This boldly textured scarf design by Emma Sewell (UK) uses a combination of double and single cloth, together with crepe silk and linen in the weft. The warp is also crepe silk, giving lengthways elasticity and a beautiful drape to the fabric.

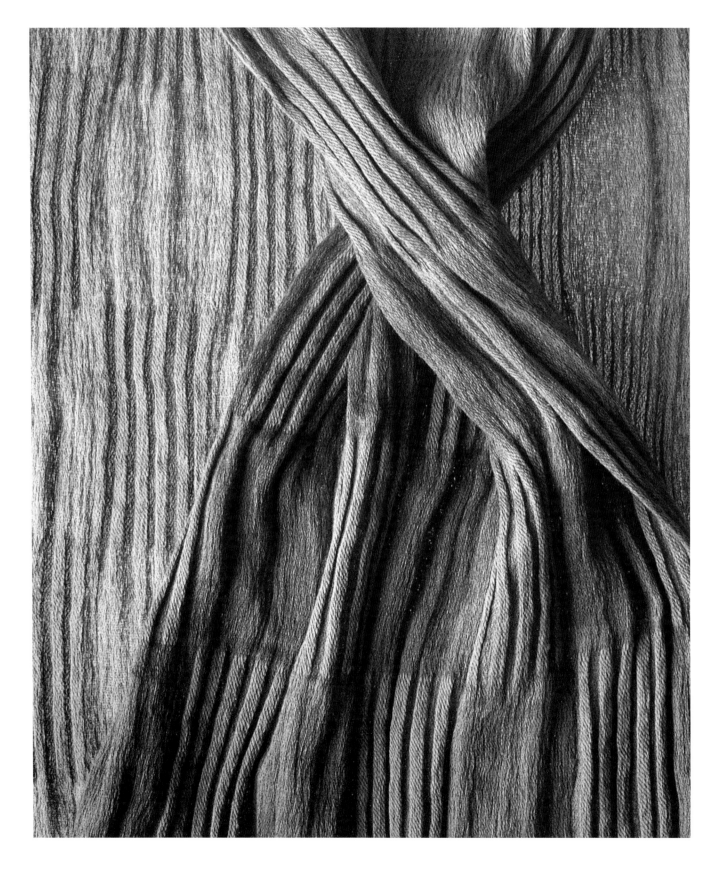

Double Cloth Combined with Double-sided Structures

True double cloth can also be combined with other double-sided weaves to increase the range of variations for colour, texture and pattern within the fabric (as in the piece shown opposite). A particularly useful combination is double plain weave with 3/1 twill, because these structures have two intersections in common (both warpways and weftways). This increases the number of pattern blocks that can be produced, allowing more varied designs to be woven on relatively few shafts. If alternate ends are threaded on shafts 1 and 2, then only two shafts are required for each pattern block, giving three blocks on an eight-shaft loom (as shown in the draft below). This principle can, of course, be extended to more shafts, giving five blocks on twelve shafts and seven blocks on sixteen shafts. Structures using this very useful style of threading are sometimes known as double two-tie unit weaves: refer to Barrett and Smith, 1983, for a very thorough treatment of these structures.

Other Combinations of 'Shared' Structure

The combinations of three-span floats, shared by double plain weave and 3/1 twill, also occur in warp-faced compound tabby, but only in the warp direction. So these structures could also be used together to create the same number of blocks as 3/1 twills, though they will require more lifts than the double/twill combination, and so are not so useful for treadle looms.

Doing More with Layers

The design possibilities of double-faced and multilayer cloths are so wide that this has necessarily been a very brief survey. Any of the areas that I have touched upon could form the basis for years of work and innumerable designs. However, the combination of a single layer together with multiple layers within the same cloth seems to offer particularly wide scope for experiment, and is one of the design strategies that will be looked at in the next chapter.

OPPOSITE:
'Pleat Chequerboard' scarf. Blocks of double plain weave are combined with both 3/1 and 1/3 twills (using the warp-float/weft-float stripes described in Chapter 5). The weft consists of eight picks S, eight picks Z, of a fine crepe silk, but the texture it creates varies according to the weave structure. In the double plain areas, the different twists 'fight' one another to create a crepe texture, while in the twill blocks they 'co-operate' to create a pleated effect. Warp: Linen. Weft: Crepe silk.

RIGHT:
If alternate ends are threaded on shafts 1 and 2, then only two extra shafts are required for each pattern block, giving three blocks on eight shafts.

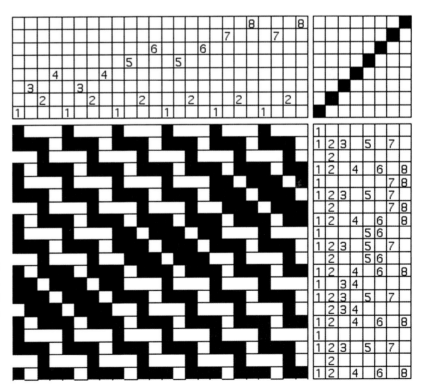

CHAPTER 7

TEXTILES THAT SHAPE THEMSELVES

The techniques discussed so far are creating overall textures in what are essentially rectangular pieces of fabric. But it is also possible to vary the yarn and/or weave structure from one area of the fabric to another, to give different fabric qualities and amounts of contraction, so that pieces woven as rectangles will be transformed in shape during wet finishing. For example, Ann Sutton has experimented with triple cloths, playing off yarns of different shrinkage against one another, and interlacing the layers in varied ways, so that they tug at one another, pulling the fabric out of its rectangular shape.

The possibilities for fabric shaping range from simple changes in width, which produce attractive flared borders or rippling selvedges, to more complex variations of yarn or structure, which may cause the finished pieces to assume many different shapes. These techniques can be applied very effectively to scarves or shawls, but they have particular potential for garments, which may be woven so that they can go almost directly from loom to body (by way of wet finishing, of course) with little or no cutting and minimal stitching. These

shaping techniques also work extremely well for textile jewellery and accessories. For example, Junichi Arai uses a combination of single, double and quadruple cloths to create a bag that can be simply cut from the loom as a finished object. This chapter will consider several different ways in which shape can emerge.

The finished reversible bag. The splitting of the cloth into quadruple layers creates a very open sett, which allows high-twist weft to escape between the warp ends, creating a bouclé surface.

A bag by Junichi Arai. Weaving starts with a single layer of cloth and a normal weft yarn, forming a firm base for the bag and avoiding the need for a stitched seam. The fabric then becomes a quadruple cloth, woven with a high-twist weft, creating a narrower patterned tube. The weaving then switches to two layers of very soft cloth, separate at the selvedges, which will allow ties to be inserted into the bag. A further section of quadruple cloth is woven, and then a final strip of single cloth. The bag is cut from the loom and turned inside out. The ties are inserted and one half of the bag pushed into the other.

This triple cloth by Ann Sutton, one of a series of six, has an interchange of cloth layers, using linen and two different wools, to reveal the varied shrinkage potential of the yarns. This group of pieces was part of her 'No Cheating' exhibition, which explored the idea of wide experimentation, while always playing within the rules of weaving.

Z and S Twist for Fabric Shaping

When using high-twist yarns in both warp and weft, very different patterns of texture will emerge, depending whether warp and weft are the same twist (Z × Z or S × S) or have opposite twists (Z × S) (see Chapter 4). These contrasting textures also produce different amounts of fabric contraction, because the deep undulating waves of the Z × S interactions take up more fabric than the flatter textures produced by same-twist interactions. These differences can be emphasized by using a twill weave, where opposite yarn twists cross one another, and plain weave for same-twist interactions. Examples were given in Chapter 4 of how the contractions of these differently textured blocks could create curving lines within the fabric. However, these different textures could also be exploited to shape entire pieces of cloth in a similar way.

The situation when working with a normal-twist warp and high-twist weft is different. If using one direction of twist to produce a crepon effect, the amount of contraction produced by Z or S yarns will be the same. However, the different twists can also be alternated in stripes of varying width, and this *will* affect the extent to which the cloth can contract. The narrower the stripes, the more the different yarn twists will 'fight' one another, so different textures can be produced, ranging

LEFT:
S × Z twist interactions, in a 2/2 twill, create an undulating texture that causes extreme fabric contraction compared with the more modest shrinkage produced by S × S interactions, in plain weave.

RIGHT:
'Curve' scarf. Z and S yarns are used for warp stripes that become progressively narrower across the fabric. These stripes decrease in size from a few centimetres in width at one edge (giving a crepon effect), to alternations of 2 Z, 2 S (giving a crepe effect) at the other edge. As the crepon texture can shrink more strongly than the crepe, these twist variations shape the fabric. Warp: Crepe wool, Z and S. Weft: Spun silk.

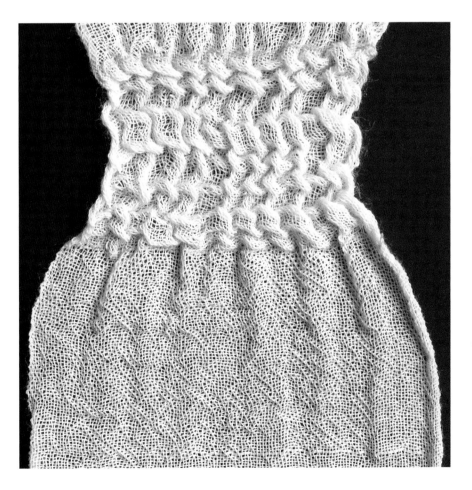

119

In this subtly shaped scarf by Noriko Matsumoto, high-twist wool and linen are used as wefts throughout, but the way they are combined changes. This allows different amounts of shrinkage along the length of the piece and alters the density of the fabric, so that its translucency also varies. (Photo: Noriko Matsumoto)

Woven as a double-cloth tube, this collar is shaped so that it sits comfortably and stays in place on the shoulders. The technique of shaping is similar in principle to that used for the 'Curve' scarf, though this time the crepe yarns are in the weft. The top part of the fabric is woven with Z-twist weft, and narrow stripes of S-twist yarn are then brought in, alternating with Z stripes of gradually decreasing size. The cloth in its loomstate is shown at the bottom.

from a strongly contracting crepon to a less tightly shrinking crepe (*see* Chapter 4). A transition can be made within a fabric, gradually decreasing the width of stripes across the warp, so that the fabric is able to shrink less at one selvedge than at the other. Similar techniques can, of course, be used weftways.

High-twist/Low-twist Shaping

Fabric shaping can also be achieved through combining high-twist and normal-twist yarns in various ways. Even if these contrasting yarns are used throughout a fabric, shaping can be produced if they are combined in different ways in different parts of the cloth, as in the work of Noriko Matsumoto (see example opposite). However, high-twist yarns may also

be used in only some parts of the fabric, and contrasted with normal yarns in other places, much as is done to create a seersucker texture (*see* Chapter 4) but used more gradually, or over larger areas, so that the fabric itself becomes shaped. This could be a steady transition, gradually substituting non-shrinking for shrinking yarns, to give a gentle flare to a fabric. Alternatively, for a more dramatic shaping effect, a sudden juxtaposition of the different yarns can be very beautiful, particularly if relatively stiff materials such as linen or metal yarns are used to create a strong contrast. Examples are shown overleaf, by two different designers. Dörte Behn, who uses such juxtapositions to great effect, has written eloquently on the importance of a sense of structure and an appreciation of material properties in the production of truly 'Intelligent' textiles (refer to Behn's 'Intelligent Textiles – The Originals', *see* Bibliography).

121

Dörte Behn (Germany) explores the possibilities of double cloth and different materials in her elegant series of 'Trumpet Scarves', playing off high-twist weft yarn against linen, to create a range of beautiful shapes. (Photo: Jürgen Liefmann)

An exuberantly textured neckpiece by Lucia Schwalenberg, which plays off shrinking and non-shrinking yarns against one another. (Photo: Heiko Preller)

This neckpiece by Lucia Schwalenberg (Germany), in silk, wool crepe and copper, makes dramatic use of the contrast between shrinking and non-shrinking yarns. (Photo: Heiko Preller)

123

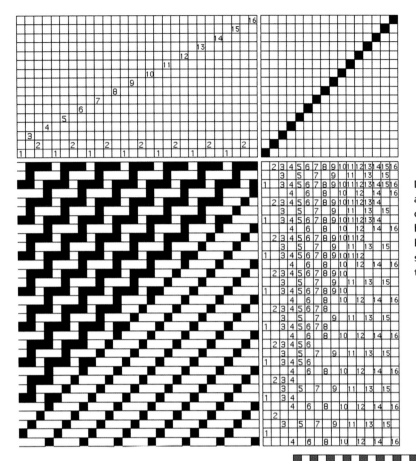

Double plain cloth combined with 1/3 twill. If alternate ends are threaded on shafts 1 and 2, then only two extra shafts are required for each pattern block, giving seven blocks on sixteen shafts. If a high-twist weft is used, this will allow gradual fabric shaping through differential shrinkage between the two structures.

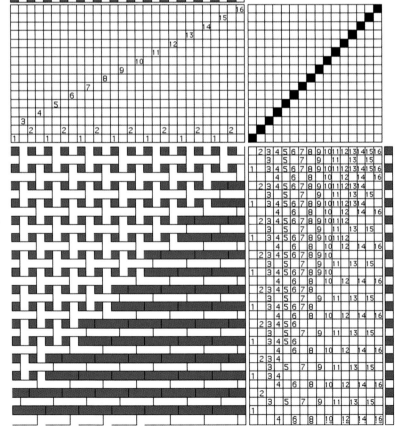

Double plain cloth combined with 1/3 twill, shown as a colour diagram. If contrasting colours are used for the two plain cloths, these combine in the twill areas to form colour-and-weave effects, in this case a horizontal hairline stripe. The other face of this fabric will show a dark plain cloth combined with vertical hairline stripes.

'Doublecloth Loop' scarf. This can be interlaced around the neck in a variety of ways, and has a border that is shaped through changes in weave structure, while the weft yarns remain the same throughout. The arrangement of blocks is similar to that in the drafts opposite, except that double plain stripes have been inserted between the twill blocks. Warp: Linen. Weft: Crepe wool.

Varying the Structure for Shaping

Another strategy is to keep the yarn the same but change the weave structure. Different weaves will vary in their ability to contract, depending on how closely interlaced they are, and these differences can be used to shape the fabric. For example, double plain weave will contract more than most single cloths (see Chapter 6), and these differences can be exploited to create shape. This can be used either for sudden changes of shape, through a sharp transition of structure, or for more subtle ones, since by gradually changing the proportions of the two weaves across the cloth, the potential for contraction will be progressively changed. Different single-cloth structures also have different capacities for contraction so many variations are possible. The combination of double plain weave and 3/1 or 1/3 twill (described in Chapter 6) is particularly useful for this type of shaping. It allows a number of blocks to be produced on relatively few shafts, so it is possible to shape a fabric very gradually, by progressively changing the relative amounts of double and single cloth.

A group of sample pieces experimenting with fabric shaping ideas for garment designs, using various combinations of material. There are several different arrangements of double cloth and 1/3 or 3/1 twill, and an example of double cloth combined with warp-faced compound tabby (centre top).

The three-span floats shared by double plain weave and 3/1 twill also occur in warp-faced compound tabby, at least in the warp direction, so this combination of fabric structures could also be used for gradual fabric shaping. Other weave combinations that vary in shrinkage potential could be used in a similar way, particularly if they are simple structures, able to give many pattern blocks on relatively few shafts. For example, the alternating float weaves, discussed in Chapter 5, require very few shafts for each block, and combine well with plain weave, allowing gradual changes in cloth contraction to subtly shape the fabric.

Structure Reversals for Shaping

Structures that create pleated effects, such as warp-float/weft-float stripes, or alternating cords, depend on a reasonable amount of fabric being woven to allow the effect to develop fully. In Chapter 5 I warned against too frequent reversals of such structures, to avoid flattening the texture of the fabric. However, context is everything, and a technique to be avoided in one situation may be ideal in another. Such frequent reversals provide another way of shaping a fabric.

Yarn Thickness Changes for Shaping

Gradually changing the thickness of the weft yarn is yet another way to shape the fabric, when using warp-float/weft-float stripes. The combination of a thick warp and a fine weft is a good way to create pleating (*see* Chapter 5), but as thicker wefts are used the pleated effect tends to become weaker and may eventually be lost altogether. Once again, something that is best avoided when simply aiming for a textured piece of fabric, can be seen to come into its own when creating a shaped piece – gradually substituting thicker wefts can be an effective way of creating a flared shape (*see also* Chapter 10).

Putting Things Together

Each of the last few sections has focused individually on a different method of creating shape. But this is to simplify things for the sake of explanation – in the real situation of designing, you may wish to use several techniques at once. The contrast between high-twist and normal-twist yarn can be emphasized very effectively through the choice of materials, or by

This sample shows how reversals of 3/1 and 1/3 twill stripes can shape the fabric. If a few centimetres are woven between reversals, the fabric still pleats tightly, but with very frequent reversals, the fabric starts to flatten out. The weft remains the same throughout. Warp: Spun silk 60/2 Nm, 60 epi. Weft: Spun silk 210/2 Nm, 60 ppi.

also bringing in a change of structure. For example, Eileen Hallman (1999) has described how she shapes clothing by using three different combinations of material and structure, to give a gradual transition from wide to narrow. The main body of her fabric is a single cloth, either plain or twill, in normal yarn. She then weaves a transition area in the same structure, but using a high-twist handspun yarn. The final, shrinking section of the fabric is woven in double plain cloth with the same high-twist yarn. Such different combinations create a subtle gradation of shape, and many combinations of technique could be used in a similar way. For example, reversals of structure would be enhanced by also changing the thickness of the yarn, and so on. If aiming for a really extreme change of shape, you may need to draw upon all your resources.

Further Experiments with Twist and Structure

In the last three chapters I have given a brief survey of some structures and strategies that are useful when working with high-twist yarns and/or strong contrasts of material. Of course there are many other possibilities, but my aim has been simply to give a general sense of the factors to be considered when using weave structure in this context. As well as the structures that have been traditionally used to create texture, there are many others that can be put to good use in this way. Just as the integrated cell weaves, which started life as colour-and-weave effects, have become popular structures for creating texture, there are many other traditional pattern weaves that can be used in new ways. Those that include both plain weave areas and long floats (for example overshot weaves, distorted warp or weft effects and spiders) seem to offer particular scope for textured effects. For example, Anna Champeney (2009) has experimented in precisely this way, using high-twist yarns with standard overshot weaves to create textured scarves (refer to her article in the winter 2009 *Journal for Weavers, Spinners and Dyers* – see Bibliography).

More complex structures, relying on many shafts, network drafting or Jacquard looms, also offer opportunities for creating pattern on fabrics that are textured by high-twist yarns, or for creating texture by means of the structure itself, through differential shrinkage. Complex patterning techniques also have great potential for creating shaped pieces of cloth because they can allow extremely gradual changes in the fabric to give very subtle shaping. There are plenty of books that cover weave structures in detail, and many traditional weaves deserve to be looked at afresh in the light of their possibilities with high-twist yarns (*see* Bibliography).

Good industrial texts on weave structure include the classic books by William Watson, *Textile Design and Colour* (the 7th edition has recently been reprinted), and *Advanced Textile Design*. Other out-of-print industrial texts worth looking out for are Nisbet's *Grammar of Textile Design*, Strong's *Foundations of Fabric Structure* and Robinson and Marks' *Woven Cloth Construction*. Good books are also available, specifically aimed at handweavers. A thorough account of a broad range of weave structures is given in Sharon Alderman's *Mastering Weave Structures*, together with sound advice about drafting your own designs. Madelyn van der Hoogt provides detailed coverage of many traditional weaves, including overshot and lace weaves, in *The Complete Book of Drafting*, while Ursina Arn-Grischott provides an extensive and beautifully illustrated account of double cloths. Ann Sutton's *The Structure of Weaving*, with beautiful photographs by David Cripps, is now unfortunately out of print, but it is well worth searching for a copy. The companion volume *Ideas in Weaving* (co-authored with Diane Sheehan) is still in print, and although not specifically focussed on structure as such, is full of stimulating examples of fabrics. Details of these and other useful books are given in the Bibliography.

In this sample of warp-float/weft-float pleating, the pleated effect fades out as the thickness of the weft is gradually increased. The influence of yarn stiffness can also be seen, through the comparison of hard silk (stiff because it still retains the gum) and softer degummed silk. The hard silk (seen at the top of the picture) is not forming such good pleats in this case. However, it does give more body to the fabric than the degummed silk, and so might be a very suitable weft to be used for wider pleats. Warp: Spun silk 60/2 Nm, 54 epi, linen 77 lea, 72 epi. Weft *(top to bottom)*: Hard silk 60/66 denier, 56 ppi; degummed silk 60/66 denier, 56 ppi; spun silk 210/2 Nm, 50 ppi; spun silk 120/2 Nm, 40 ppi; spun silk 60/2 Nm, 30 ppi; spun silk 30/2 Nm, 26 ppi.

CHAPTER 8

PRACTICAL TECHNIQUES FOR HIGH-TWIST YARNS

From a practical point of view, high-twist yarns can pose some problems in handling. The extra twist that gives such interesting effects in the finished fabric may sometimes cause the yarn to snarl up in an annoying way during warping, beaming and threading or when winding bobbins. However, these problems can usually be kept under control by taking a little extra care, and making a few modifications to normal techniques. A complete account of setting up a loom will not be given here, since excellent instructions are given in many other weaving books. Instead, my emphasis will be on identifying points in the process where some modification of normal technique is desirable to take account of the special properties of high-twist yarns. Some of these methods should also prove useful when handling normal yarns that are very fine and delicate. See the box opposite for some general recommendations about things to avoid.

Active, high-twist yarns in the warp make a strongly textured fabric with lengthways elasticity, which has been elegantly swathed around the body to create this 'Cleopatra' dress. Fabric design: Lotte Dalgaard (Denmark). Garment design: Ann Schmidt-Christensen (Denmark). (Photo: Ole Akhøj)

Working with High-twist Yarns in the Warp

THINGS TO AVOID

When working with high-twist yarns in the warp, *do not*:

- Warp the loom 'front-to-back'. See **Warping and Setting Up**.
- Tie threads of different twist directions together. *See* **Winding the Warp**.
- Wind the warp on through the raddle without inserting a stick for clearing. See **Beaming**.
- Pull forward several ends when threading. *See* **Threading the Heddles and Reed**.
- Tie threaded or reeded ends in very small bundles. *See* **Threading the Heddles and Reed**.
- Tie reeded bundles of yarn tight up against the reed. *See* **Threading the Heddles and Reed**.
- Tie the cross sticks tightly together. *See* **Weaving**.
- Tie the cross sticks to the back of the loom. *See* **Weaving**.
- Use techniques in samples that will be impossible full scale. *See* **Weaving**.
- Keep on weaving samples without cutting off and finishing to get feedback. *See* **Weaving**.

If kinks of yarn are wound into the warp, they will untwist later
and cause slack ends during weaving.

Enclosing cones in 'socks' can subdue lively yarns.

Warping and Setting Up the Loom

The method that I recommend is to wind the warp on to the back beam, using a raddle to space it, before threading the heddles and reed. Two crosses should be made in the warp: a raddle cross to allow the warp to be distributed in the raddle, and a singles cross for threading the heddles. Details of this method (sometimes referred to as 'back-to-front') are described in many standard textbooks; Peggy Osterkamp gives a particularly clear and detailed account in both her books (*see* Bibliography). Sectional warping is also an option, as this keeps yarns under tension and prevents them from tangling.

'FRONT-TO-BACK' WARPING

Note that the method of warping the loom 'front-to-back' (as is commonly done in the USA) is definitely *not* recommended for these difficult yarns. It offers too many opportunities for them to become tangled.

Of course, if you are a devotee of 'front-to-back' warping, you may be reluctant to give up this method. But if you decide that you really must wind on the warp in this way, then it is very important to take much more care than with normal yarns, and to try to keep the yarn under some tension whenever possible, to avoid tangling. I do also strongly recommend giving the 'back-to front' method a serious try.

Winding the Warp

Work slowly and carefully, watching out for any snarls in the yarn – take care to untwist them because they will cause trouble if they are wound into the warp. They will untwist themselves later when the warp is on the loom, and cause individual ends to become slack.

Yarns vary in their liveliness, and some that have rested on cones for some time (or been steamed or sized at the factory to subdue them) may be manageable enough for multiple end warping. With others that show a strong tendency to snarl, it is usually quicker in the long run to warp with a single end. Crepe wool can often be handled quite easily, with a little care, but crepe silk is always much more lively. If a yarn is causing trouble, then it needs to be drawn off under a slight tension, and there are various methods of doing this. With small yarn packages, simply putting the package on its side in a spool rack, and pulling against the weight of it, can provide this tension. Larger packages which are too heavy for this treatment, can be enclosed in an elastic tube. The special 'socks' supplied to machine knitters for restraining lively yarns are ideal, but an old pair of nylon tights also works well. If you use this method, keep the crepe packages permanently in their socks, as these are also needed when winding yarn on to bobbins. When saving old nylon tights for this purpose, it is useful to keep both the 'leg' and 'body' parts so that you can deal with different sized cones. The sock should only fit closely enough to gently restrain the yarn as it is pulled from the cone – a very tight sock can generate so much friction that the yarn becomes *more* lively, rather than less!

Other ways of getting a light tension on the yarn can also work well. Lotte Dalgaard frequently uses high-twist yarns as warp, particularly in her fabrics designed for garments (*see* chapter opener). She has devised a very effective approach to getting some tension on the yarn while warping, by slowing it down on its way to the warping mill. This can often be done simply by wrapping it around some of the pins on a spool rack, but Lotte has also set up a special board fitted with a varied series of loops, through which the yarn can be interlaced in many different ways, and this allows for a very subtle adjustment of tension. Her book *Magical Materials to Weave* (*see* Bibliography) gives a detailed account of such a set-up.

TYING YARNS TOGETHER

Note that it is important to be aware that tying together high-twist yarns of *different* twist directions – that is, tying a Z yarn to an S yarn – may cause breakages, as these yarns tend to *untwist* one another. It is therefore best to test yarns, before you start making the warp, to see whether this will happen (some commercial crepes that have been steamed to set them may be stable enough to be tied together). To be on the safe side, it is preferable to tie off one yarn and tie on the new yarn separately. It is also best to avoid tying together yarns with very different amounts of twist, to avoid 'leakage' from the higher twist one.

ONE WARP OR TWO?

If you are planning a large project in which you will be mixing different types of yarn or different weave structures, it is important to find out, at the sampling stage, whether it is going to be possible to combine these within a single warp. Sometimes odd combinations will work well on short warps or if you can cut off regularly – for example, between scarves – but it is vital to note any difficulties during sampling if you are intending ultimately to weave a very long length where tension problems could build up.

It is not only high-twist yarns that may cause problems. Other interesting yarns that work well in textured fabrics may also cause difficulties due to their uncompromising character. Stiff materials, such as linen or silk/steel, make attractive fabrics when crossed by high-twist wefts, but they will tolerate relatively little variation in tension and this makes it difficult to combine structures that take up differently. However, sometimes an apparently difficult combination will be successful if one of the yarns is very forgiving (for example, spun silk with silk/steel). The important thing is to try out various methods of dealing with awkward combinations of yarn or structure at the sampling stage, before committing yourself to a full size warp that could cause difficulties.

Sometimes it will become clear that different yarns really must be tensioned separately. The ideal is obviously to use two warp beams, but if you have only one beam on your loom, there are other ways of varying the tension. A good, simple method is to insert a stick under the yarns that are expected to become slack. As weaving progresses, this stick can be pushed down on to the warp beam and weighted to take up the slack. This technique is also useful as an emergency measure if tension problems arise unexpectedly. An alternative is to make two warps but to leave one of them unbeamed, and hang it off the back of the loom, still chained and weighted to provide tension. In this case, think carefully about which of the warps should be on the beam, where it will have better control. For example, if mixing linen and silk, beam the linen and chain the silk. If mixing normal and high-twist yarns, it is usually best to beam the high-twist warp. However, this decision will also depend on the relative quantities of yarn: for example, if one of the warps is only providing occasional narrow stripes, then whatever it is made of, it may well be better to chain and weight that one.

'Spiral' neckpiece. The warp used for this neckpiece combines silk/steel in plain weave, with spun silk in a cord weave. Surprisingly, this combination of different materials and structures can be run from a single beam. Although the silk/steel is an extremely unforgiving yarn, which will tolerate no tension variations, the spun silk is very accommodating. In contrast, the same combination of plain weave and cord, using silk/steel throughout, quickly becomes impossible to weave.

Beaming

Winding the warp on to the beam does not usually cause serious problems, provided the warp is kept under tension, but remember that high-twist yarns are more prone to tangling than normal yarns, so they can easily become jammed in the raddle. A useful technique, described by Lotte Dalgaard in her book *Magical Materials to Weave* (*see* Bibliography), is to insert a stick over and under individual raddle groups. This stick can be slid forwards gently to clear any tangles before the yarn is wound on through the raddle. The advantage of this method is that any resistance due to tangles can be *felt*, so that it is possible to stop and avoid breaking the yarn (by contrast, if the warp is simply wound through the raddle, then by the time a tangle is noticed, these delicate yarns may already have broken). In Denmark, this warp-clearing stick is supported by long sticks, laid from the front to back beams on each side of the loom (these are also used for supporting the cross sticks and later the reed while setting up). Alternatively, the clearing stick can be suspended from the sides or top of the loom.

Threading the Heddles and Reed

These threading processes are usually fairly straightforward, though high-twist yarns do tend to tangle with one another more than normal yarns. I suggest fastening a bunch of the warp yarn to the cloth beam or the side of the loom using a lark's head knot, so that the yarns are under tension. Then gently pull threads out of this bundle for threading through the heddles. Usually it is best to pull out no more than two threads at a time (one in each hand works well, to prevent them tangling with one another). If the yarn is very lively, it may be necessary to pull out only one thread at a time. As each group of yarns is threaded, tie them in fairly large *loose* bundles with a slip knot (avoid small, tight bundles as these may later be difficult to undo).

Threading the reed usually causes no special difficulties. Hanging the reed in a horizontal position, from the top or side of the loom frame (rather than placing it upright in the beater), makes things easier when working with difficult yarns. Although traditional reed hooks are perfectly adequate, automatic reed hooks (autodenters) are extremely efficient and convenient, especially for threading fine reeds. These hooks are specially constructed so that they move automatically from one dent to the next. As the yarns are threaded, tie them loosely in bundles about 2.5cm (1in) wide using slip knots. Once the reed has been threaded, it can then be placed in the beater.

The warp of this fabric is mainly of fine linen, in an open plain weave, but it also has narrow stripes of a thicker linen yarn in a backed twill and with a closer sett. These yarns and structures take up differently, and since linen has little elasticity the two sets of yarns need to be separately tensioned.

An automatic reed hook (autodenter) is a useful tool that makes threading the reed quick and easy, especially with fine reeds. The reed is hung in a horizontal position for threading (rather than being placed upright in the beater), and as the autodenter is pushed up, it moves automatically from one dent to the next. It also has a small flange that prevents it from falling out of the reed.

Tying On

The most efficient method is to *lace* bundles of yarn to the front stick. This technique is fundamentally very simple and works extremely well, but does require a little care, so please read the following instructions *carefully* before you start. Sometimes, after a quick glance, people assume that they know what is going on. They may then fail with the method because they have not really understood it.

- When the reed has been threaded, all the yarn should be in loosely tied bundles of about 2.5cm (1in). Before starting to tie on, undo each of these in turn, and pull and flick at the yarns to make sure there are no loose threads or tangles. Then tie each yarn bundle once again with a slip knot, as near to the end of the yarn as possible, to avoid waste.
- Take a length of smooth cord and tie it to the front stick. Pass the cord down through the centre of the first bundle of yarns, then back under the stick, down through the next bundle and so on, until all the bundles of yarn have been laced to the stick.
- Tie the end of the cord firmly to the front stick. The tension can then be adjusted evenly across the warp, using the cord. If the yarn bundles are reasonably even in length, a cord about six times the width of the warp will usually be adequate for lacing, but if the bundles are very uneven, or you have chosen to tie bundles that are much smaller than 2.5cm, then allow extra cord.
- When tying a wide warp, the lacing cord will need to be quite long, so it is best to wrap it into a butterfly, to make it easy to handle.

It is *very important* to ensure that the tension is *evenly distributed* while the warp is *still quite slack*, and then to tighten it only gradually. When people fail with this method of tying on, it is usually because they have made the warp very tight, while the bundles are unevenly tensioned, and have *then* tried to distribute the tension – this will not work! So tighten the ratchet just a few notches and then push down firmly on each bundle of yarn and flick gently at the lacing cords to encourage slippage – loose bundles will give up their slack to tighter ones, so that the tension gradually becomes more even.

Go through this process repeatedly, gradually tightening the ratchet and distributing the tension until the whole warp feels firm and even. This is a quick and efficient method that

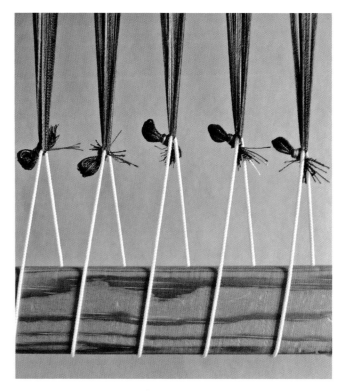

Lacing the warp to the front stick is an efficient method of tying on that reduces loom waste. Though essentially simple, this technique does need to be done correctly, so follow the instructions carefully to ensure success.

cuts down on warp waste. It is also much easier than the traditional method of tying the warp yarn directly to the front stick, where every attempt to tighten one part of the warp seems merely to loosen the warp at some other point! With the lacing method, the physics of the situation is actively *helping* you to achieve a more even tension.

It is best to use slip knots for the yarn bundles when tying on a new warp, in case any threading errors are found, since these knots can easily be untied to make a correction. If an error is found, it is not necessary to disturb the whole tie-up, but *only to untie the bundle with the error*. When this has been corrected, the warp tension must be slackened off to allow the bundle to be retied *around* the empty loop of cord that has been left on the front stick. The warp should then be gradually tightened and the tension across the whole width checked and readjusted if necessary. If you cut off during the weaving process and need to retie, then the lacing can be done even more economically by using overhand knots, once you know that there are no errors and if you are sure that you do not want to change the sett. However, when using overhand knots on very slippery yarns, take care to tie them *very* tightly and not too close to the ends of the yarn bundle, otherwise a knot can gradually slip to the end of the yarn and come undone.

Weaving a Header

When you start to weave, use some spare yarn, rather thicker than your intended weft, to space your warp. The most efficient method is to throw across several picks *without* beating, and then to beat these down as a group – the friction created, as the weft threads bind together, distributes the warp threads evenly. When working with delicate warp yarns, do this cautiously at first to avoid breakages – throw two picks and gently beat them down together. If you can feel that there is not too much resistance, then try beating down three picks together, or four. Repeat the process several times. This will spread and space the warp much more quickly than simply starting to weave in the normal way. The method is also useful for picking up any individual ends that are loose, and bringing the slack to the front of the warp.

Once the warp has been spaced in this way, it will be easy to see if the tension is even, since the weft threads should lie straight across the warp. One of the great advantages of the lacing method is that, even at this stage, it is very easy to adjust the tension. If any of the warp bundles are too slack (weft bulging upwards) or too tight (weft dipping downwards), then adjustments can be made to the lacing cords until it is clear that an even tension has been achieved.

Weaving

High-Twist Yarns as Warp

After all the problems of preparation, weaving itself is usually relatively straightforward. Many high-twist yarns are not as strong as normal yarns (the high twist puts them under stress) but should give no trouble as warp if they are treated with reasonable care and not put under too high a tension. It is desirable to keep the cross sticks in the warp during weaving, partly to be able to quickly and correctly replace broken ends, but also to keep warp tangles well back from the heddles. However, the sticks should *not* be tied tightly together, and must *never* be tied to the back of the loom. Such techniques, which are often applied to smooth, 'easy' yarns, are a recipe for disaster with high-twist yarns. It is best to leave the cross sticks separate from one another and after each advance of the warp move them carefully back, one at a time, gently clearing any tangles. Rather than being tied to one another, the sticks can be individually suspended from the top of the loom, or attached to the side, depending on the design of the loom. This will prevent them from slipping out when the tension is released to advance the warp, and will also stop them from falling and pulling the warp out of the heddles, if you cut off during weaving.

High-Twist Yarns as Weft

As weft, high-twist yarns usually cause few serious problems – the pull of the bobbin in traditional side-delivery shuttles is generally enough to prevent them from snarling. The best method of winding bobbins is to wind the yarn to within 1.5cm (¾in) of the ends of the paper quill or spool and then gradually decrease the traverse to make a rounded shape. It is *very important* to move the yarn back and forth along the bobbin fairly quickly, so the successive layers lie *criss-crossed* over one another – upper layers of yarn are thus prevented from cutting into the lower layers and making the bobbin unstable.

End-delivery shuttles are also very effective for high-twist yarn, but need careful tension adjustment, and for crepe silk may also need to be lined with fur, to prevent yarn from springing off the pirn and filling the shuttle cavity. Several manufacturers are now producing end-delivery shuttles for handweavers, but it is also worth looking in antique shops for old powerloom shuttles. Although some of these may be too large and heavy, smaller ones work very well as hand shuttles. The metal points are rather sharp for comfortable handling, but it is easy to file these down to make gently rounded ends. Often these shuttles have only a simple exit hole for the yarn, with no tensioning device, but a good tension can be achieved by making a *plug*. Take a small bunch of yarn and wrap it tightly around one end to form a miniature 'tree' that can be inserted into the shuttle to control the tension of the yarn. If you make a few of these of different sizes, then it is possible to get good control over a variety of yarns.

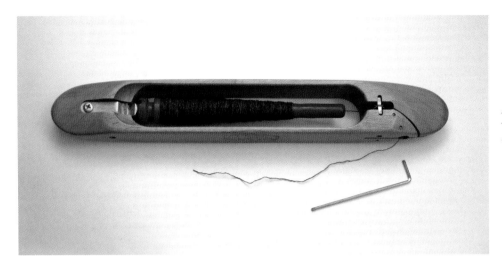

An end-delivery shuttle, designed for handweaving. The yarn tension can be adjusted using an Allen key.

An old powerloom shuttle, lined with fur and with a plug in the exit hole to control the yarn tension. A paperclip can be adapted to make a convenient hook for pulling the yarn through the exit hole.

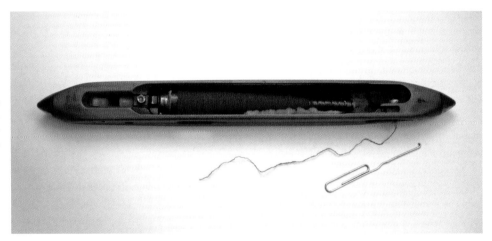

Detail of end-delivery shuttle, showing a plug in place, and another in the foreground. The plug is like a miniature tree, whose 'branches' are pushed into the exit hole of the shuttle.

Weft Sett

It is very important to attend to the sett (picking) of the weft when working with high-twist yarns, both during the design process and when making full-scale pieces. While you are at the design stage, it is essential to be rigorous about recording the sett of your samples. Use a linen tester to check the ppcm (ppi), and make sure you write this down. You will need this information to be able to reproduce the same cloth quality on a larger scale. Very open setts are often desirable with high-twist yarns, so it is important to learn how to beat lightly – weavers are generally so used to beating hard, that beating very lightly can be quite a challenge, but you will not create any textured effects if you do not allow your yarns sufficient room to move. It may help to close the shed before beating to create more resistance to the beater. Also, take care to keep an *even* beat – large variations can obviously cause changes in the cloth's ability to develop texture, and this is particularly important when weaving a long length, perhaps over many days or weeks. It is best to check, from time to time, that you are not gradually drifting away from your intended sett. Also, the very open sett that is often necessary makes weft slippage likely, so use plenty of sticks or paper when winding the fabric on to the cloth beam.

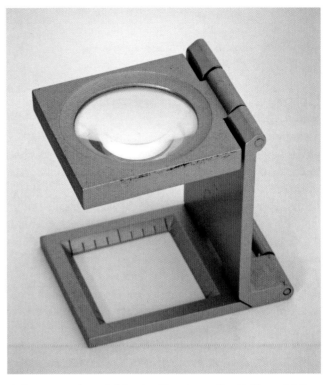

A linen tester is useful for checking the weft sett. These folding magnifiers are designed so that, when unfolded, they are the correct distance from the cloth. The most useful ones are marked in both centimetres and inches.

Samples in Relation to Full-scale Pieces

One point that needs particular care is the way the weft is laid in the shed while working on small samples. Weavers are usually advised to lay the weft at an angle, or in an arc, to allow adequate weft for take-up, to avoid the cloth drawing in excessively. This is good advice in general but needs to be used thoughtfully. If you lay the weft at a large angle, say 30–40 degrees, in a sample that is only 15cm (6in) wide, there is no way that you will be able to replicate these conditions on a much wider piece of cloth. Even with the beater pushed well back, the weft can only be laid at an angle of 10–20 degrees on a wide warp, so there will be less weft going into the cloth. This will tend to pull the warp threads closer together in the finished cloth, effectively increasing the warp sett, possibly so much that textured effects begin to be reduced.

This probably accounts for the difficulty some weavers have described in achieving good textured effects on wide cloths. It has been reported that narrow pieces are successful, but with wider warps, the texture is less prominent in the centre of the cloth than at the edges. This is particularly likely to happen if the weaver lays the weft in an arc, rather than at an angle, since the reed will strike the top of the arc first, pushing the weft yarn out to the sides, so that the cloth is looser at the edges than in the centre. To avoid such problems, aim to do nothing at the design stage that will not be physically possible on a larger scale. So, when sampling, try to lay the weft at a realistic angle in relation to the width of fabric you finally wish to make. Alternatively, if you are working from existing samples where you may have laid the weft in at a relatively large angle, you might consider using a slightly more open warp sett to compensate when you weave a wider piece.

Another important aspect of sampling is that it is essential to keep cutting off pieces and finishing them in order to get feedback. The design process needs to be a thoughtful 'conversation' between you and the material, and this aspect of design will be discussed in more detail in Chapter 10.

Using a Stretcher (Temple)

Although a high-twist weft will not shrink violently until it is wetted, there is often still a noticeable tendency for the cloth to draw in, and in this case use a stretcher to support the cloth and avoid excessive wear on the selvedges. This also helps with the problem described above, of losing texture with wide pieces of cloth, since the cloth will be held out at the correct sett, as the weft is thrown across it. There seems to be a widespread prejudice that using a stretcher is a sign of poor technique, but this is to misunderstand the nature of cloth. As the warp and weft yarns bend around one another, the woven cloth is bound to draw in to some extent, and this will vary depending on the sett and combination of yarns. Many traditional cloths were fairly closely woven, with a fine, tightly spun warp and softly twisted, bulkier weft that filled the spaces between the warp ends, and such a combination should cause relatively little draw-in of the cloth. This seems to be the basis of the idea that weavers 'ought' to be able to manage without a stretcher. With crepe fabrics, the situation may often be quite the reverse. A warp yarn, with a very open sett, may be crossed by a high-twist yarn that is equally fine (or even finer), leaving plenty of space between the warp ends. As the yarns crimp around one another, this combination is very likely to cause cloth draw-in. This is not bad craftsmanship – just physics. So get out those stretchers when necessary, and don't feel guilty about it!

Finishing

Stabilizing Techniques

High-twist yarns readily curl, crinkle and escape from the weave, so it is best to stabilize any cut edges (especially where high-twist yarns have been used as warp) as soon as possible, and certainly before wet finishing. Since most of these fabrics are openly set they would, in any case, be naturally prone to fraying, but the lively nature of high-twist yarns definitely makes this worse. Twisted fringes can be a good solution if

high-twist yarn has been used as warp, but hemming may also work well in some designs. In this case it is best to use a sewing machine to zigzag the cut edge as soon as possible to stabilize it, and then turn it under and stitch again to form a proper hem. If the high-twist yarn is only in the weft, things are a little easier. In the case of scarves that are to have a fringe, a few picks of waste yarn should be woven in to prevent fraying, and the piece can then be washed. Edge finishes are discussed in more detail in Chapter 10.

Wet Finishing

A warm wash, using a mild detergent to encourage water penetration, will develop most textured effects. Some commercial crepe wools, which have been steamed to set the twist, come with a manufacturer's recommendation for finishing at 60°C. Although this high temperature is very effective at triggering the yarn to crepe rapidly, it is not essential, since the reaction is due to the absorption of water rather than heat as such, and will still take place with cooler water, though more slowly. Only when using heat-sensitive synthetic yarns is it essential to use high temperatures (see Chapter 9). The disadvantage of finishing at 60° is that it is necessary to wear rubber gloves to handle the fabric. My personal preference when working with traditional crepe yarns is to use hand-hot water so that I can handle the fabrics with my bare hands. It is then easier to manipulate the fabric as necessary, for example pulling the fabric warpways or weftways to encourage pleating. Sometimes a fabric is rather slow to react and needs to be gently rolled between the hands to provoke the creping reaction.

Light fulling can also be used with wool fabrics if they do not seem stable enough after washing. High-twist yarns themselves tend to resist fulling, but yarns that full more readily could also be included in a fabric to improve its handle or other properties. For example, if a very smooth yarn in an open sett is showing a lot of slippage, it may help to include some softer twist yarn that will full easily and give the fabric more stability. The way that yarns of different character react to the fulling process can also be exploited as part of a design. An interesting example is given by Anne Field in her book *Collapse Weave* (pp. 110–111, see Bibliography) in which she has used warp and weft stripes of two different yarns: an alpaca, which develops a strong tracking pattern (see Chapter 4), and a softer wool yarn, which does not. These differences were emphasized by a finishing treatment in the washing machine, which left the tracking pattern of the alpaca blocks still clear, while the blocks of softer wool yarn had begun to felt.

Given the different character of the wool fibres from the various breeds of sheep, together with the great variety of levels of twist applied to different yarns, differential fulling clearly offers plenty of scope for experiment. The technique has been put to particularly imaginative use in the work of Gilian Little, who makes dramatic use of the contrast between a high-twist yarn and a more softly twisted, easily fulled yarn (see examples illustrated overleaf). Combined with a multi-layer weave structure, this results in a most unusual fabric. A design such as this relies partly on the interaction of different twist levels with the process of fulling. However, even without high twist, fulling can create interesting textures by using wool yarns together with other fibres that resist fulling (*see* Chapter 9).

After washing, the maximum texture and elasticity will usually be achieved by letting the fabric dry without any tension on it, for example by laying it out on an absorbent surface such as cork. If either the warp or weft is a normal-twist yarn, the finish may be improved by pinning out the fabric under a light tension in this direction, though whether this is desirable will depend on the design – experiment on samples if in doubt. If allowing high-twist yarns to relax completely does not give a satisfactory finish, the fabric can be pinned out under tension to give the desired effect, but remember that a fabric finished in this way will *shrink to its 'natural' dimensions* if washed.

For small items, such as scarves, an alternative method of drying is very effective for pieces with a definite warpways pleat. Take a piece of soft cord or ribbon and loop it round the end of the scarf with a lark's head knot. The scarf can then be suspended and left to drip dry. The cord does tend to leave a slightly crushed area, but this will recover if damped slightly.

Finishing Crepe Silk

Crepe silk may need special treatment, as the yarns often still retain the sericin or natural gum (silk in the gum is known as raw or hard silk), which gives the fabric a very crisp handle (over and above the crispness imparted by the high twist). This can produce an attractive, lively cloth quality, but it may sometimes seem too harsh for certain purposes, particularly with heavier weights of crepe silk. Some or all of the silk gum can be removed from the cloth by boiling in soap solution

or other suitable detergents, and this is the normal finishing treatment used in industry. The process is progressive: 30–45 minutes will soften the silk considerably, but an hour or more may be necessary to remove the gum completely.

When a crepe fabric is wet finished, the silk gum slows down the absorption of water and the subsequent swelling and shrinking of the creping reaction. For this reason, the texture ('crepe figure') produced in traditional silk crepes is very fine and even. Only after this reaction has taken place is the fabric degummed to give a softer texture. When rayon was first used as a substitute for silk in the industrial manufacture of crepes, it was found to produce a disappointingly coarse and uneven crepe figure because water penetrated too quickly, and swelling and shrinkage occurred very suddenly. It became necessary to size the rayon yarn before twisting in order to simulate the effect of the silk gum, and so slow the penetration of water to obtain a satisfactory result.

Fabrics woven with hard silk show interesting variations in texture when they are wetted out and when they subsequently dry. When a fabric is first wetted out, the texture may initially appear fairly large in scale, but as the water penetrates completely over a period of a few minutes it becomes progressively finer and the fabric will shrink considerably. If it is degummed at this point, then this fine texture will be retained. However, if you choose to leave the gum on the silk, an interesting reaction occurs as the fabric dries out. A piece of creped cloth that has contracted strongly and become very finely textured will expand as it dries and form a larger-scale texture than it had while wet. This might, perhaps, seem a reasonable expectation for all crepe yarns; if wetting imposes an extra stress on a high-twist yarn, then drying obviously removes it, so one might expect the yarn to partially uncurl. However, this reaction occurs to only a slight extent with wool or cotton. It seems likely that variations in the stiffness of different yarns may be the key factor here.

Crepe silk that retains the gum is very stiff, but once it has absorbed water, its texture is considerably softened and this must allow a very small-scale pleated texture to develop within the fabric when it is thoroughly wetted. When water is lost as the fabric dries, the yarn stiffens again, and this, combined with the reduction of stress, probably gives the yarn the capacity to unbend and produce a larger-scale texture. A similar reaction is also seen with linen and paper (other stiff yarns that soften in water), though the effect is less strong than with silk. It is possible that crepe silk in the gum possesses a unique combination of stiffness and elastic recovery.

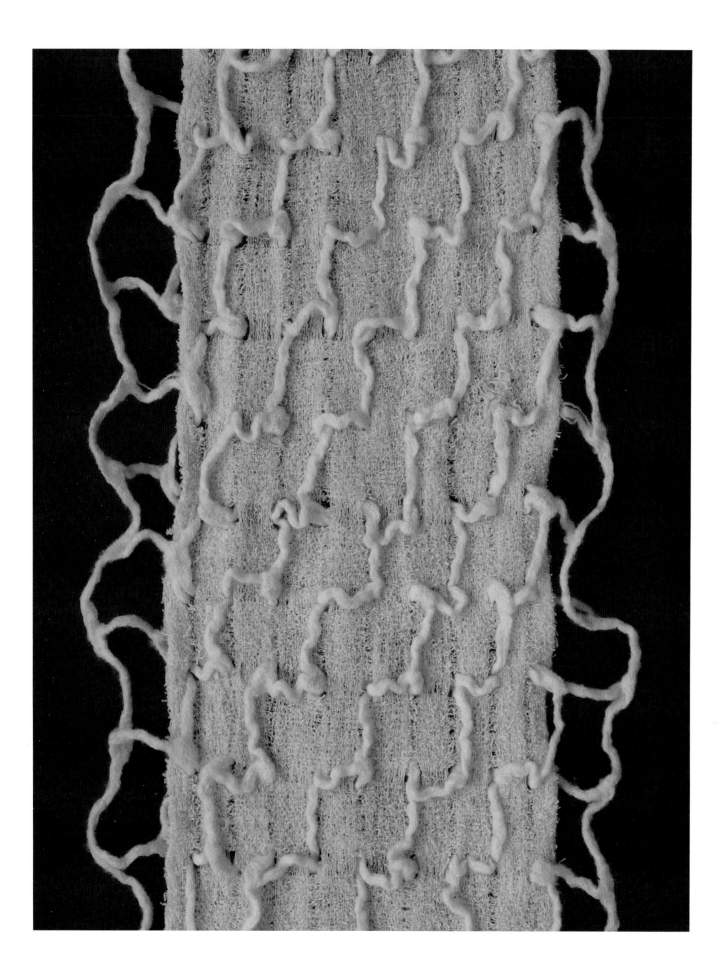

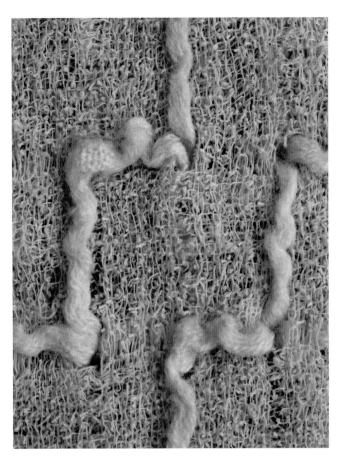

This close-up shows the contrasting textures of the two types of yarn.

OPPOSITE:
In this complex, multilayer scarf by Gilian Little (UK), the crinkled surface produced by high-twist wool is contrasted with the very different texture of a wool yarn that fulls easily. The two sets of yarns, with their distinctive qualities, interlace with one another in a most intriguing way. The strong shrinkage of the high-twist yarns also leaves the easily fulled yarns free to form a dramatic edge to the scarf. (Ann Sutton Collection)

Comparison of identical samples of fabric with silk crepe weft, immediately after washing (with the sample still wet) and after subsequent drying. *Top*: Whilst wet, the fabric has a tightly crinkled texture. *Bottom*: After drying, the texture has become larger in scale and the fabric has expanded in width. Both S and Z wefts have been used. The beige colour of the Z yarn (the top half of each sample) is an identification tint, so that the different yarn twists can be easily distinguished. Warp: Linen 44 lea, 32 epi. Weft: Crepe silk 4 × 40/44 denier, 32 ppi.

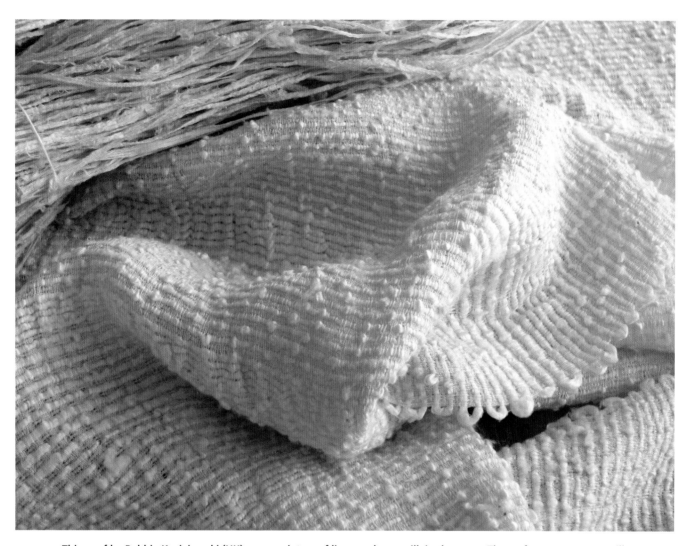

This scarf by Bobbie Kociejowski (UK) uses a mixture of linen and spun silk in the warp. The weft yarns are crepe silk and silk string, both of which retain the gum, making the piece very stiff in the loomstate. The scarf has been partially degummed to give a moderately soft texture. The spun silk in the warp has not been adversely affected by this modest treatment, and in this case preserving a very high lustre has not been a major issue, since the texture created by the contrast of silk string and crepe silk is the main focus of the design.
A skein of silk string is visible in the top left-hand corner of the picture.
(Photo: Bobbie Kociejowski)

Because silk that retains the gum is so stiff, the finished fabric may be quite crisp. If, after a fabric has been washed and dried, you feel that it is too crisp, it can of course be wetted out again and degummed. However, it is wise to test the effect of degumming on small samples before committing yourself to treating a large piece. Remember that the crinkling of the yarn will become finer in scale as the yarn loses its stiffness. Any pleats that have developed in the fabric while the yarn retains the gum will become smaller in scale and may possibly lose definition if the gum is removed. Also, there is the issue of the effect of degumming on other yarns in the fabric.

Degumming usually works well if the fabric is composed entirely of hard silk or where the crepe silk has been used together with linen or cotton. But if crepe silk is combined with spun silk yarns (which have already had the gum removed) it is best to proceed cautiously and perhaps to experiment with just a partial treatment, as the alkaline solution can reduce the lustre of the yarn. This may or may not be a serious problem, depending on whether the lustre of the spun silk is important in the design. Wool can also be adversely affected by hot alkaline solutions. In some cases it may be better simply to leave the gum on the silk, and although such fabrics may initially seem a little harsh, they do soften gradually with wear and repeated washing. Also, although softness is usually considered a virtue, sometimes a fabric is actually improved by the body given to it through retaining at least some of the silk gum. Bobbie Kociejowski has experimented with different degrees of degumming and has told me that, for some of her scarf designs, she has found that the optimum effect can be achieved through a partial degumming.

Undyed crepe yarns often have an identification tint, indicating S or Z, which is to help avoid mistakes during weaving, since these yarns are usually so fine that it would not otherwise be possible to distinguish between them at a glance. In the case of crepe wools, these 'fugitive' tints wash out easily, but with crepe silks they tend to be rather resistant, though they will be removed if the silk is degummed. If the silk is to be left in the gum, then the presence of the identification tint may give a faint colour cast to the finished fabric, particularly in the case of white fabrics. If this spoils the effect of the cloth, then the identification tint can be removed with a hot ammonia solution.

Piece-dyeing and Cross-dyeing

When working with undyed crepe yarns, especially silks, *piece-dyeing*, which involves dyeing the finished piece of cloth, is a useful technique (*see* Chapter 4). It is often claimed that silk must be degummed before it can be dyed, but this is a popular misconception and it is perfectly easy to dye silk that retains the gum. If a finished fabric is to be dyed in this way, there is no need to remove the identification tint, unless very pale colours are to be used. Work out the dye recipe based on the amount of yarn that will take up the dye. In the case of a fabric that is entirely silk or wool, this will be the whole cloth, which can simply be weighed. However, if you are cross-dyeing (*see* Chapter 4), only some of the yarns will take up the dyestuff and it is necessary then to calculate the amount of yarn involved. However, some of the dye will temporarily attach itself to the other yarns and will need to be removed by boiling in a mild detergent at the end of the dye process. It may also be necessary to increase the amount of water used, to be able to completely immerse the cloth. For these reasons it is, in practice, often difficult to follow a normal dye recipe precisely, in the sense of being able to state the percentage of dyestuff that has been taken up by the yarn. The important thing is always to record exactly what you actually did, so that even if your recipe is not entirely accurate in conventional terms, it is still possible to replicate it.

RECIPES

For 100g of cloth: if the fabric is only partly raw silk, calculate the required soap and other ingredients based on the weight of the silk yarn. It may then sometimes be necessary to increase the amount of water slightly to ensure that the cloth is fully immersed. This will obviously reduce the concentration of the soap, so making it difficult to follow the recipe precisely. Always keep careful records of what you actually do, so that even if a recipe is not precise in conventional terms, the procedure can be replicated.

SILK DEGUMMING
2ltr water
10g soap
Immerse the cloth and boil for up to 1 hour, until the silk is softened. Rinse in warm water.

TINT REMOVAL
2ltr water at 60°C
2g soap
8ml household ammonia
Immerse the cloth and leave for 15–20 minutes. Rinse in warm water.

Additional Techniques for Modifying the Fabric Finish

The advice given so far is based on the idea of emergent effects in which different fibres, yarn twists and structures spontaneously interact to create texture, when wet finished. However, although these effects are very powerful in themselves, it is also possible to apply additional techniques to modify the result. Mention has already been made of metal yarns, which give fabrics a temporary 'memory' for moulding by hand (*see* Chapter 5). This extra shaping can give a further dimension to fabrics that are already strongly textured.

Another reason for applying modifications is that textures produced entirely with high-twist yarns often give a rather random effect. Although this is part of the charm of these techniques, it may sometimes seem desirable to intervene to control the way that the force of the yarn is released, to create more orderly textures. This is sometimes done in industry with rayon crepes, which may be embossed with a texture before wet finishing, to achieve a more even crepe figure. The embossing does not in itself *create* the final texture, since this is still due to the contraction of the crepe yarns, but it does *direct* the way that the energy of the crepe yarns is released to give a more consistent result.

Some handweavers have also experimented with such modifying finishes. For example, a 'woven shibori' technique can be used, in which gathering threads are inserted during the weaving process. When the fabric is removed from the loom, these gathering threads are drawn together to impose a pattern of texture, and the fabric is then washed and dried before the gathering threads are removed. Fabrics may also be steamed or boiled to increase the permanence of the texture. Such techniques are often simply used with normal yarns, but some weavers are also combining this technique with the use of crepe yarns, so that these provide the force to create the texture, while the shibori technique determines precisely where the energy of the yarns is released. Woven shibori can be very effective when applied to the whole fabric, but interesting results can also be produced by using it only in some areas, while other parts of the cloth simply develop a natural texture.

OPPOSITE:
A fabric by Lotte Dalgaard, with linen warp and crepe wool weft. A woven shibori technique, followed by steaming, has been used to create sharp pleats. The energy of the crepe yarn provides the force to pleat the fabric, but the woven shibori directs where this force will be applied. (Photo: Ole Akhøj)

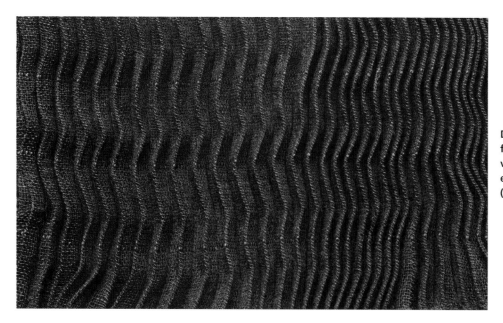

Detail of a woven shibori pleated fabric by Lotte Dalgaard. Colour variations have been used to emphasize the edges of the pleats. (Photo: Ole Akhøj)

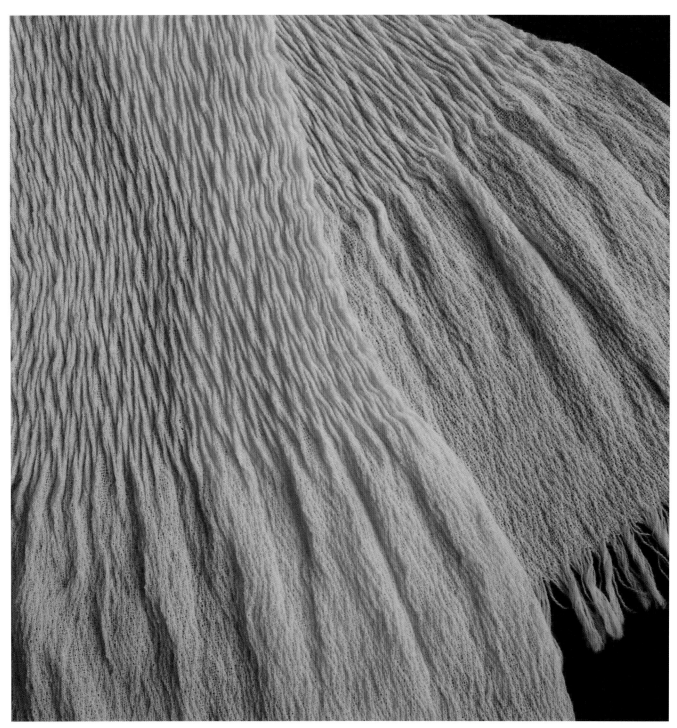

OPPOSITE:

A pleated scarf by Teresa Kennard, woven in 3/1 and 1/3 broken twill (*see* Chapter 5). The natural pleat has been modified in some areas with woven shibori and the scarf has then been dyed. This technique creates an interesting contrast between softly pleated areas, which are evenly dyed, and sharp pleating, where the dye has taken only on the edges of the pleats. Warp and weft: Spun silk.

ABOVE:

A scarf by Teresa Kennard (USA), using woven shibori as a modifying finish. Warp: Wool. Weft: Crepe wool, with S and Z twist alternating for the border, to create a natural crepe effect, and a single direction of twist for the body of the scarf, where the shibori technique has been applied.

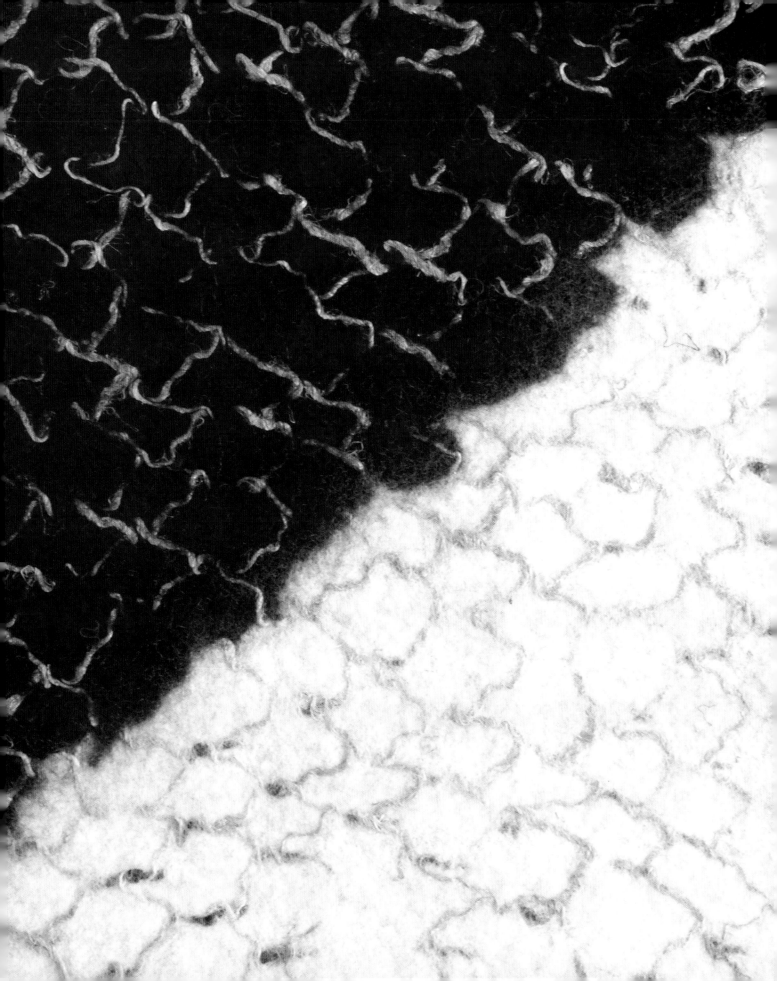

CHAPTER 9

TEXTILE CONNECTIONS

This book has focused on textured effects in woven fabrics, and mainly on those produced using high-twist yarns. However, there are various related methods that offer considerable scope for experiment, through using different materials or other textile techniques. Some of these create highly textured fabrics, while others result in more subtle effects, but all share the property of being emergent processes that produce complexity through the interplay of simple elements. As I have relatively little personal experience with most of these techniques I will not attempt a detailed account, but I would like to draw attention to them briefly, and to some of the designers and artists who are working with them.

Synthetic Materials

The use of high-twist yarns to create textured fabrics goes back thousands of years, but over the past century, many new synthetic yarns have been produced that can be very effective in creating textured fabrics, using some of the weave structures that have already been described. However, their properties do differ from those of high-twist yarns, and this needs to be taken into account. These synthetic yarns fall into two groups: elastomeric yarns, containing materials such as elastane (Lycra); and heat-sensitive shrinking yarns, made of materials such as polyester or acrylic, which shrink when treated with hot water or steam.

When wet finished, the elastomeric yarns shrink along their length, sometimes developing a fine crinkled texture, rather than exhibiting the definite spiral movements characteristic of high-twist yarns. Consequently if used alone, they do not give the distinct surface textures such as crepon that high-twist yarns create so well. However, they can give very bold surface effects if they are combined with other yarns, as in the work of Liz Williamson (*see* Grace Cochrane's book *Liz Williamson: Textiles*, *see* Bibliography). They are also excellent in float weaves, where a strong contraction of the yarn is an advantage. Elastomeric yarns retain their stretch properties in the finished fabric. Lotte Dalgaard gives a good account of these materials in her book *Magical Materials to Weave* (*see* Bibliography), with useful comparisons of their properties with those of high-twist yarns. She provides detailed suggestions on the handling of these sometimes rather difficult yarns. Anne Field also gives helpful practical advice (in *Collapse Weave*, *see* Bibliography) and shows a range of examples of fabrics woven with elastomeric yarns, including interesting shaped pieces where these yarns are played off against normal yarns.

The heat-sensitive synthetic shrinking yarns give a very different fabric quality. They respond to heat by shrinking along their length but without developing a crinkled texture, and they have no elasticity after the heat treatment. Consequently, although they can produce strongly textured effects, the resulting fabrics are firm in handle, without elasticity.

In this wall hanging, Gusti Austin Lina (Netherlands/UK) has used heavy fulling to emphasize the contrast between wool and linen. The loosely woven linen has become bonded to the wool, creating delicate waves that ripple through the fabric.

This double-cloth scarf by Junichi Arai, with cotton warp and weft, also includes a polyurethane elastomeric yarn in the weft. The pleated effect develops because gaps are left in the warp in both layers, so that the yarn shrinkage is concentrated along these lines. Arai excels at creating bold effects by ingeniously simple means. (Ann Sutton Collection)

A scarf by the Nuno Corporation, in which an elastomeric yarn is used as weft across only part of the fabric width. This creates a heavily textured central section that is played off against the flat borders of the scarf.

RIGHT:
This fabric by Lotte Dalgaard uses a heat-sensitive shrinking yarn of wool and acrylic, combined with 'Jet Tex', a non-shrinking polyester yarn. When treated with water at 80°C, the wool/acrylic yarn shrinks to create a raised texture.
(Photo: Ole Akhøj)

'Torque': the spiral form of this neckpiece arises from the contrast between a paper yarn and a synthetic heat-sensitive shrinking yarn. Warp: Paper and 'Body' (a viscose/polyester shrinking yarn). Weft: 'Body'.

'Curve', a scarf by Liz Williamson, in which a woollen yarn that shrinks is combined with a wool/polyester blend that resists shrinking. (Photo: Ian Hobbs)

Fulling

Another method of producing texture is to exploit the fulling potential of wool using contrasts of structure, materials or both. Anne Field (in *Collapse Weave*) gives attractive examples of wool fabrics that rely on the differing fulling potential of floats and plain weave areas of cloth, while the yarn remains the same throughout. Even stronger textures can be produced if wool that fulls easily is played off against materials that resist fulling. These fabrics are generally relatively firm, without the extreme elasticity created by high-twist yarns.

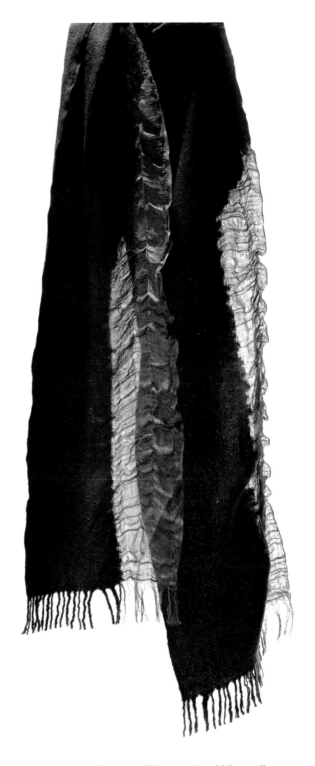

'Grey Edge', a scarf by Liz Williamson, in which woollen spun yarn is contrasted with cotton. Some of the woollen warp ends have been replaced by cotton during the weaving process to create an intriguing and beautiful juxtaposition of textures. (Photo: Ian Hobbs)

Detail of a scarf by Sheila Reimann, in which the contrast between wool and silk creates a gently bubbled effect, with random variations.

Such effects can work well entirely in wool, through the contrast between wool yarns that full easily and those that have been given special treatments to resist fulling. However, more extreme contrasts – for instance between wool and materials such as silk, cotton, linen, paper or synthetics – can be particularly effective. Lotte Dalgaard covers these techniques in *Magical Materials to Weave*, and good examples are also given by Anne Field in *Collapse Weave*. The possibilities have been very widely explored by Liz Williamson, who plays wool off against other yarns such as silk and cotton (*see* Williamson, 'Fulled Seersucker Scarves', 2002, and also the monograph about her work by Grace Cochrane, *Liz Williamson: Textiles*, 2008).

A wide variety of structures can be used in this way, combined with finishing treatments of varying degrees of rigour, from light to heavy fulling. For example, Stacey Harvey-Brown uses piqués, overshot weaves and stitched double cloths to create textured effects, by combining materials that respond differently to a finishing process of handwashing followed by tumble drying. She also exploits woven shibori techniques in a similar way (described in her book *Woven Shibori for Textural Effects*: *see* Bibliography). Many of these combinations of technique result in textured, three-dimensional effects. However, much more subtle textures can also be created through the action of heavy fulling on strongly contrasting materials, as in the work of Gusti Austin Lina (*see* chapter opener).

A textured fabric by Stacey Harvey-Brown (UK), where contrasting materials have been used in an overshot weave. The fabric has been finished by handwashing, followed by tumble drying, to develop the texture. (Photo: Stacey Harvey-Brown)

Metal Yarns as Active Yarns

Because of their stiffness, yarns containing metal can be very effective as passive yarns, giving dramatic rippled textures when they are combined with active yarns (refer to Lotte Dalgaard's *Magical Materials to Weave* for examples of this type of effect). However, there are some yarns that are constructed by wrapping a metal strip around a central textile core and these are often intrinsically unbalanced, giving a reaction, on wetting, that is reminiscent of the behaviour of high-twist yarns. It seems likely that this is indeed a true stress reaction and arises from the tight wrapping of the metal strip around the textile core. Such yarns usually have cores of rayon, or occasionally silk, and both of these fibres will react to wetting by

swelling. Since the metal strip restricts the scope for swelling, this must put stress on the core of the yarn. The way that the yarn reacts is precisely related to the direction of the metal wrapping – thus S-wrapped yarns behave like S-spun high-twist yarns, spontaneously plying themselves in a Z direction when wetted out, while Z-wrapped yarns ply themselves in an S direction.

Weaving with these unbalanced yarns can create textured surfaces that are similar to those produced by high-twist yarns. Some fabrics produced in India, with very fine core-wrapped metal wefts, are well known for their ability to develop a crinkled texture when washed for the first time. Metal yarns vary a great deal in terms of their weight, stiffness and reactivity, so that a variety of different textures are possible. These

A fabric by Junichi Arai, in which a metal weft has reacted in a similar manner to that of a high-twist yarn. As the fabric is plain weave, the texture is entirely due to random variations produced by the yarn. (Ann Sutton Collection)

OPPOSITE:
Wendy Morris (UK) has used a networked draft to create a fabric that is firmly woven in some areas and more loosely interlaced in others. This varies the extent to which an active metal weft can react in different parts of the fabric. A sample of the loomstate fabric is shown at the top of the picture. Warp: Spun silk. Weft: Wrapped metal yarn.

effects have been studied in detail by Wendy Morris (*see* Bibliography for details of her article 'Work in progress – Research into Wires and Metallics', 2010), who has experimented with a wide range of different metallic yarns and wires to create a variety of textured fabrics.

Contrasts of Fibre for Fabric Shaping

Examples have already been given of techniques for shaping fabrics using high-twist yarns and contrasting, non-shrinking materials (*see* Chapter 7). These fabrics have a textured surface and they also have elastic properties. However, similar principles can be used, but with more subtle contrasts of material, to create shaped textiles that have a smooth surface and a firm fabric quality, suitable for wall-hung pieces. Deirdre Wood uses juxtapositions of materials such as silk and linen to create rectangular pieces of fabric, which become dramatically curved when cut from the loom and finished. These techniques are described in detail in the exhibition catalogue, *Deirdre Wood: straight and narrow* (Whiting, 2005).

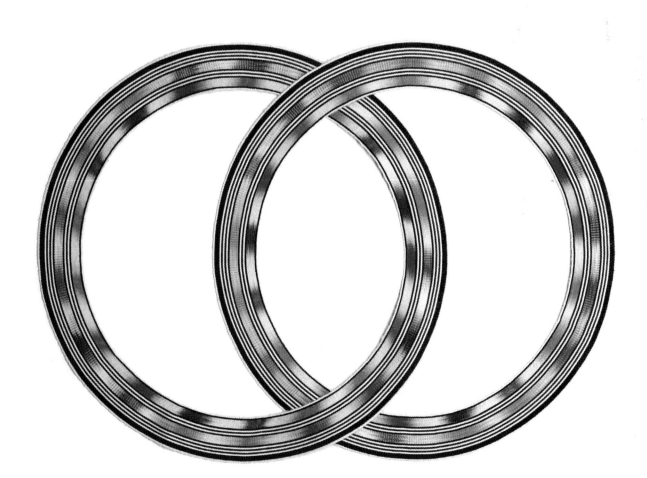

In Deirdre Wood's pieces, which are designed for architectural settings, curving stripes emerge from the contrasting properties of silk and linen. This piece is composed of interlocking circles, each of which was simply a straight strip of cloth on the loom.
(Collection of the LEE & WON Foundation, Korea; Photo: Joe Low)

Knitted sample by Alison Ellen, using high-twist yarn. The zigzag effects are produced by alternating stripes of Z and S twist yarn, while keeping the knitted structure the same. (Photo: Colin Mills)

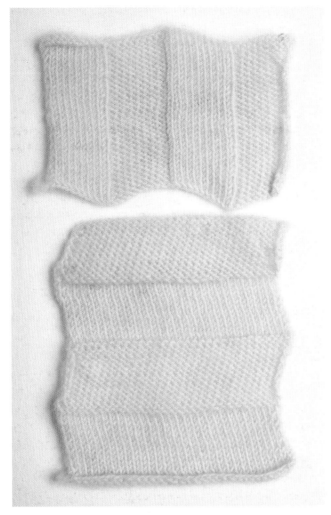

Knitted samples by Alison Ellen (UK), using high-twist yarn. The zigzag effects are produced by alternating stripes of plain and purl knitting, while keeping the direction of yarn twist the same. (Photo: Colin Mills)

High-twist Yarns in Knitting

High-twist yarns can give very striking effects in knitting. Using an unbalanced yarn for stocking stitch will cause knitting to slant, as the force of the yarn interacts with the vertical and horizontal loops of the knitted stitches on the two faces of the fabric. Knitting books will sometimes suggest avoiding such yarns to prevent this 'problem', but as usual, breaking the rules can be rather productive. A rhomboid-shaped piece of fabric results, and a particularly interesting effect arises from

using broad stripes of plain and purl knitting. In this case, the knitting will slope first one way and then the other, creating a zigzag effect in the fabric. In contrast, when garter stitch or ribbed structures are used, the alternation of stitches on the two faces of the knitting causes the forces to balance out, and the fabric no longer slopes. So there is great potential for special effects through varying the structure of the knitting to allow unbalanced yarns to cause distortions in some places, but not in others. Zigzag effects can also be produced in stocking stitch by alternating stripes of Z and S yarns. Alison Ellen is exploring the potential of these techniques, and examples are given in her book *Knitting: colour, structure and design* (*see* Bibliography). There are also possibilities for seersucker-type effects through using stripes of balanced and high-twist yarns.

Other Textile Techniques

Other techniques, such as crochet, lace making and braiding, could also be used with high-twist and shrinking yarns. Such effects do not seem to have been very widely explored, probably because these techniques have other ways of creating

'Wave Rhythms IV', a braided structure by Jennie Parry (UK), which exploits the contrasting properties of paper and silk yarns, to create a three-dimensional effect. (Photo: Jennie Parry)

shape and texture. However, this is also true of knitting, and clearly it is possible to exploit contrasting materials and high-twist or shrinking yarns, as well as traditional methods of fabric shaping. For example, the braid maker Jennie Parry has produced some striking pieces using various combinations of materials with contrasting properties, such as paper and silk, to create three-dimensional effects in her braids. She has also experimented with heat-sensitive shrinking yarns, playing these off against more stable materials. Now that unusual yarns are more readily available to designer-makers, there is plenty of scope for further experiments with various textile techniques.

CHAPTER 10

DESIGNING AS A CONVERSATION

In his book *The Reflective Practitioner*, Donald Schön discusses design, among other activities, drawing attention to the way that designers learn from experience, modifying their practice in response to their 'conversation' with the materials they are using and the problems that they are addressing. He describes this way of working as *reflective* practice:

> I shall consider designing as a conversation with the materials of a situation . . . [The designer] shapes the situation, in accordance with his initial appreciation of it, the situation 'talks back', and he responds to the situation's back-talk. In a good process of design, this conversation with the situation is reflective.
>
> Donald Schön

The delicate ribbed texture and repeating rippled projections of a Murex shell formed the starting point for this 'finned' fabric. My first thought was to weave a long narrow strip that would be cut and sewn together to form a wide cloth, with a series of selvedges projecting from the surface. However, as I worked on the idea, a more interesting solution suggested itself – to weave 'extra' selvedges into the body of the cloth itself, by inserting the shuttle several times across the cloth to complete each pick. A high-twist cotton yarn running warpways, which shrinks in finishing, is responsible for throwing the extra selvedges into a rippled texture.

In a similar vein, Anni Albers emphasizes the need for the designer to have *direct* experience of a medium, seeing this as an important justification for the continued existence of the crafts in an industrial age:

> For it means taking, for instance, the working material into the hand, learning by working it of its obedience and its resistance, its potency and its weakness, its charm and dullness. The material itself is full of suggestions for its use if we approach it unaggressively, receptively.
>
> Anni Albers

This idea is very different from the view of design as something 'preformed', a drawing or 'blueprint' that will subsequently be executed precisely in the chosen medium. Design as a reflective practice is an *emerging* process, requiring the designer to be constantly responsive and adaptive in relation to the material, seeing apparent setbacks as opportunities to learn and improve the design. Bridget Riley makes a similar point, in relation to painting:

> As the artist picks his way, rejecting and accepting as he goes, certain patterns of enquiry emerge. His failures are as valuable as his successes in that by misjudging one thing he confirms something else, even if at the time he does not know what that something else is.
>
> Riley, 1997

Referring to the artist Mondrian, she suggests that, although he may fail in certain intentions, there is a sense in which he never *makes mistakes*, since everything is of use in his

The overlapping scales of a pine cone sparked off the idea for this fabric with a structure of staggered Bedford cord.

Collections of objects can provide both visual and textural ideas.

development. This is a valuable idea to keep in mind when you feel that a piece of work has gone badly wrong. Your 'conversation' with the material will certainly sometimes involve being told, rather firmly, what it will not do, but although disappointing at the time, this is a chance to understand more about the material and its properties, and is a crucial part of the process through which the design gradually emerges, as initial ideas are reconsidered, modified and developed in the light of experience.

Starting to Design

There are many different ways of initiating a design. Ideas may often arise from looking at existing textiles or working directly with materials and techniques. Alternatively, the design process may begin with a clear conception of a finished piece of work, an image in the mind's eye, or perhaps a specific commission or problem to be solved. In these cases, the designer can immediately begin to move forwards through the interplay of initial ideas and the response of the materials and techniques.

However, the starting point for a design may also come from outside textiles, in the form of observations of natural or man-made objects, which offer ideas about colour, texture and structure. Sometimes an object will provoke a strong idea, seeming immediately to suggest how it might be used. On other occasions, it is possible to feel very much attracted or intrigued by something, but unsure how to use it. Researching your subject through looking, drawing, making collages and yarn wrappings, or taking photographs, will allow ideas to emerge. Even if you are not a skilled draughts-man, the process of drawing helps you to look closely and observe accurately. Rather than aiming to make a 'finished' drawing of a complete object, it is often more helpful to concentrate on particular details where there are interesting contrasts of texture or colour – simple marks on paper will enable you to remember what you have seen and help you to organize your thoughts. Collections of objects – shells, pebbles, feathers and suchlike – which you can handle as well as look at, are also particularly useful when designing with texture in mind.

Although there can be varied ways of initiating the design process, these differing approaches cannot remain separate for long, tending instead to flow into one another. If your starting point is observational work, the constraints of material and technique will quickly begin to influence the process. Sooner or later you will be drawn into the 'conversation' of reflective design. On the other hand, if you begin with a technique that you wish to explore, the results will often trigger connections in your mind that are worth following up with observational studies or other forms of research. So, be flexible in moving between these different approaches, and be willing to break off from working on the loom at any point in the design process, to gain more information from other sources.

For strongly textured textiles, such research may benefit from being structural and functional as well as visual, and this is an approach I frequently use myself. As a former biologist, my work has often been guided not just by how natural objects look, but also by the way they are formed and how they work. Over the years I have based cloths on shells, the pleated structure of insect wings, and even the 'elastic seersucker' structure of bats' wings, a fabric that required an exceptionally highly twisted yarn (*see* Chapter 3).

Hertel's book, *Structure, Form, Movement*, which uses biology as a source of ideas for engineering, includes an interesting account of the dragonfly wing. Flat areas of wing are linked by a series of joints that are all similar in form, but which alternately face one way or the other, causing the flat planes of the wing to bend back and forth, forming a pleated structure. This has obvious analogies in weaving (*see* Chapter 5), but my initial samples for a pleated fabric based on this idea did not work as I had visualized. The fine silk weft yarns I was using, in an attempt to produce a light, translucent fabric, did not provide enough stiffness to maintain the form of the pleat. When I looked again at the insect wing, I realized that

I had neglected the importance of the small struts running *across* the pleated structure, which are responsible for providing stiffness, while still maintaining a light, delicate structure. This system proved to work well in textiles, too, with occasional picks of a linen yarn allowing the combination of both delicacy and stiffness (*see* overleaf).

Such structures and processes in nature can provide useful ideas, both as starting points for design and for resolving technical problems that arise along the way. Man-made objects and practices are also a fruitful source of ideas. For example, the techniques of origami have been helpful to me both in initiating and in working through ideas for textile jewellery. An excellent book by Paul Jackson (*see* Bibliography) gives a thorough account of paper folding as an aid to design.

When you are researching ideas, it is wise to avoid homing in on a solution too quickly, to the exclusion of other possibilities – remember there is usually more than one answer. For example, if you have been studying and drawing objects which have two distinctly different sides, it is tempting to think automatically of weaving a fabric as a double cloth. But there are many ways of creating a double-sided fabric, and rushing too quickly to an obvious solution may prevent you from finding alternative and perhaps subtler and more interesting ideas. Also, though your research may often trigger ideas that can be easily achieved through familiar weave techniques, there is no need to feel constrained by these. The well known weave structures that have been built up over generations are a valuable resource, but it is important to be willing sometimes to 'start from scratch' and analyse what you are *really* trying to achieve. This can bring in fresh ideas and is especially important with highly textured textiles.

To take an example, if your idea is for the fabric to be textured in some places and flat in others, how are you going to make this happen? Using a high-twist yarn and allowing it to float in some places, but not others, could create such an effect, but there is no need to stick rigidly to standard weave structures to achieve it. So do not think about the threading, which could constrain what you might do, but simply imagine the cloth itself. Rough sketches, indicating where you might place the floats, will help you to visualize your idea more clearly. Later, a weave draft can be derived from this and adjusted to suit the resources of your loom, if necessary. I recommend that in Sharon Alderman's book *Mastering Weave Structures* you read the chapter 'Inventing Your Own Weave Structures', especially the section on 'Turning an idea into a draft' (*see* Bibliography).

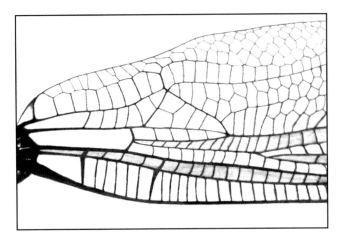

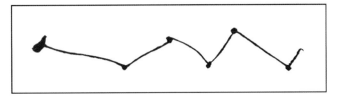

Left: Dragonfly wing.
Right: Cross-section showing the pleated structure of the front part of the wing. (After Hertel, 1966)

Detail of 'Dragonfly Pleat' fabric. A sample of the loomstate cloth is visible in the background (*see* Chapter 5 and the frontispiece for full views of a scarf made from this fabric).

RIGHT:
A classic origami fold where tensions in the paper, created by the changing relationships of mountain and valley folds, are resolved through the introduction of diagonal folds.

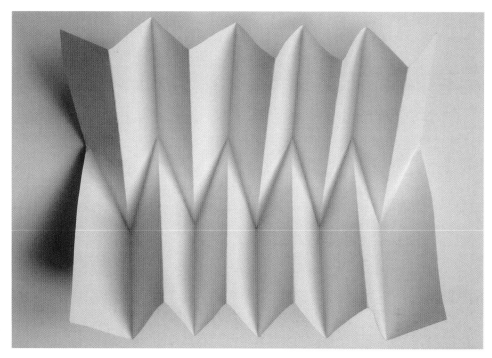

BELOW:
'Origami' neckpiece in silk, stainless steel and linen.

Getting the Most Out of Sampling

Many weavers say they dislike sampling, and some even claim that they never do it. I dispute this. If you weave a 'finished' piece without knowing how it will turn out, then this is surely simply a very large sample! In fact, sampling is vital to the design process, particularly when working with high-twist yarns and contrasts of materials, since quite small changes may sometimes cause substantial and surprising changes in the fabric. Potentially, sampling is the most exciting part of making textiles, because it is then you are most often discovering new things and really pushing ideas forwards. But it is important to know how to get the most out of it.

Why Sample?

The first thing to ask yourself is: why are you doing the sample? This may seem obvious, but it is easy to start weaving without *really* analysing what sort of information you are hoping to obtain. Of course there is a playful aspect to sampling, and there may be times when an idea is so tentative that you are simply 'feeling your way forwards' without being quite sure where you are heading. But on the whole, it makes sense to try to design samples to answer some *specific* question or to gain particular information. Thinking carefully about this before you start makes it easier to get the most out of your samples – for example, by planning to allow several ideas to be tried out on one warp. This could involve threading it on to more than the minimum number of shafts, to allow a wider range of structures to be woven, or using different setts or weights of yarn across the warp. When working with high-twist yarns, small changes in sett can make a considerable difference to the texture that is produced, so be ready to rethread the reed, maybe several times if necessary, to get the effect that you want. Remember that it is less stressful for delicate yarns if the warp is wider on the back beam than at the reed, rather than the other way round, so it will make sense to spread the warp to the widest setting that you are likely to use.

Keeping Records

Keeping records is vital. Everyone thinks they will remember what they have done, at least for a short time, but no one does. Record all basic information – materials, warp sett, reed, fabric width, structure, width of any stripes – when you first set up a sample. Then when you start weaving, write down what you do as soon as possible – preferably keep a notebook beside the loom, so that you can record the weft yarn, weft sett and length of each sample as you weave it (use a linen tester to check the sett at intervals). *Remember the weft sett is just as much a specification of the cloth as the warp sett.*

When you have cut off and finished your samples, label them as soon as possible (before you forget which one is which). The style and complexity of your labelling system is a matter of personal preference, but remember that a rough and informal system that you actually use is preferable to something more formal and impressive that you never get around to. If your labelling system is fairly basic (as mine is), make sure that you mark your samples to refer back to your notebook that contains the full specifications.

Cutting Off and Finishing Frequently

It is easy to lose some of the benefit of sampling by weaving sample after sample, without cutting off and finishing them, to get feedback on how successful they have been. This is absolutely the antithesis of reflective practice. How can you decide what to try next, if you don't know what has happened so far? Weavers are often reluctant to cut off because of wasting yarn through tying on again, but the lacing method (*see* Chapter 8) wastes very little yarn. It is much more wasteful, both of materials and time, to weave many samples that later prove to be uninformative. It is more productive to cut off after only a few samples have been woven (or maybe even only *one*, if the idea you are testing is somewhat speculative), because it is then possible to respond quickly to what has happened and make changes accordingly.

Turning a Structure During the Design Process

Another, often neglected, aspect of sampling is that it is not essential to sample a structure warpways, just because that is how the final piece is intended to be. It can sometimes be more informative or convenient to weave a sample 'sideways', in relation to the way that the final piece will be woven, particularly if there is a limited choice of yarn. For example, there are far fewer crepe yarns available than 'normal' yarns, so when planning a scarf with a passive warp and crepe weft, there may be advantages in sampling with the crepe yarn in the warp, so that a wide variety of different passive yarns can be tried across it, to see which is best. You can then turn the arrangement round when you are ready to set up the final piece, using the most successful passive yarn as warp.

It can also be worth experimenting both ways, by using a yarn or structure warpways for the first warp, but then later setting up a weftways version for a subsequent warp. This enables you to understand the design very well, and also to try a wide range of different combinations of yarns and setts before coming to a final decision. Sometimes it will become clear that both arrangements have their advantages for different pieces of work. Of course there are sometimes limitations to this process: structures that rely on tension variations in the warp cannot be precisely replicated weftways, and certain yarns, particularly the silk crepes, can be difficult to handle as warp. However, most structures can be turned, and many high-twist wools and some cottons are reasonably easy to use as warp.

Two versions of the same idea, carried out warpways and weftways. The curved scarf on the right has crepe wool in the warp and spun silk in the weft. The tubular collar has a spun silk warp and crepe wool weft. Both rely on graduated stripes of different twist directions to create shape (*see* Chapter 7).

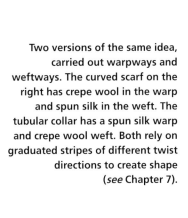

Designing Edges

Once your samples have progressed to the point where you are getting some good ideas for a finished fabric, it is time to consider the selvedges. It is all too easy for these to become something of an afterthought, when you are focusing on designing the main body of the fabric. In the case of pieces that are not simply yardage but will be complete items in themselves, such as scarves, the treatment of the raw edges is also an issue. If you leave these problems until you are almost ready to make a full size piece, then you may have to begin sampling all over again in order to resolve them. It is much better to start thinking about selvedges and raw edges fairly early on, so they can be designed in relation to the rest of the cloth. Do you want these edge treatments to be subservient to the main cloth, to 'pick up' some aspect of it, or to be major design elements in themselves?

Sometimes no special selvedge is needed. If a weave structure produces a good edge automatically, then the fabric can simply be allowed to form a 'natural' selvedge. But often it is desirable to do more than this, for either functional or aesthetic reasons. Since the selvedge takes a lot of stress it may be worth reinforcing it in some way, for example by using a stronger or more elastic yarn. Crepe yarns are often quite satisfactory for a selvedge, but they are a little weaker than normal yarns and so, to make life easier, something stronger could be used to make a more reliable edge. For example, spun silk makes a very satisfactory selvedge for crepe wool warps and can normally be run off the same beam.

However, selvedges can be more than merely strong and neat – they can be attractive and interesting. In the case of yardage, the functional aspect of the selvedge is obviously the most important. But for finished items, such as scarves, the aesthetic effect of the selvedge becomes a major consideration. If there is a repeating stripe in the design, either of colour or texture, it is worth experimenting to see which will make the most effective selvedge. For example, in the case of a warpways seersucker fabric, will the shrinking or the rippled stripe make the best selvedge? Sometimes the natural draw-in at the selvedge will make a stripe appear narrower than in the rest of the cloth, particularly when using high-twist wefts. In this case you may wish to add a few extra ends to a selvedge stripe to make it appear similar to those in the rest of the cloth. Alternatively, a stripe could be made very much wider or narrower to contrast with the other stripes. If none of the existing elements of the design seems to work, then a

different, perhaps boldly contrasting selvedge may be successful.

When it comes to dealing with the raw edges of the cloth, a classic fringe finish works well in many cases, especially for scarves. A traditional twisted fringe will make a very stable and controlled finish, though a more informal edge may seem more appropriate with some designs. When making crepe or crepon scarves with spun silk or linen in the warp, it is not always essential to make a twisted fringe. Simply leaving a few centimetres of warp yarn to form a 'natural' fringe will usually prevent fraying, since high-twist weft yarns normally stay in place quite well after wet finishing. A few picks of waste yarn should be woven in to keep the weft in place while the piece is still in the loomstate, but these can be removed later, after the piece has been washed. In contrast, if high-twist yarn is used in the warp, with a passive weft, then this combination is usually much less stable. If you are planning to make a twisted fringe it will be much easier to do this before washing the piece. If you intend to leave natural fringe or to hem the piece, then it will be wise to zigzag the edge on a sewing machine as soon as possible, to prevent fraying.

TOP LEFT:
A scarf by Sheila Reimann, which has a crepe wool warp and spun silk weft. No special selvedge has been used, but the natural spiral movements of the high-twist warp give the edge an attractive ripple. The raw edge has been finished with tightly twisted fringe. (*See* Chapter 4 for a general view of this piece.)

TOP RIGHT:
In this crammed and spaced scarf by Geraldine St Aubyn Hubbard, the outermost of the plain weave stripes forms a good natural selvedge. The weft is kept in place with knotted fringe. (*See* Chapter 4 for a general view of this piece.)

BOTTOM LEFT:
A scarf with a spun silk warp and crepe silk weft, which has a natural selvedge and also natural fringe at the raw edge. A few picks of waste yarn were used to keep the crepe weft in place while the piece was washed, and these were later removed once it was dry.

BOTTOM RIGHT:
This scarf by Emma Sewell, with crepe silk in both warp and weft, has gauze (leno) selvedges – several scarves have been woven across the width of the warp and later cut apart. It also has a natural fringe that is delightfully wild! These informal edge treatments work well in this boldly textured design. (*See* Chapter 6 for a general view of this piece.)

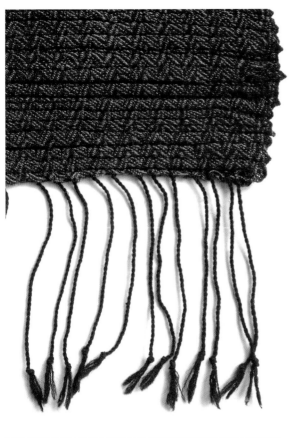

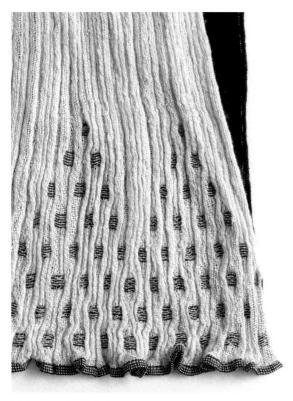

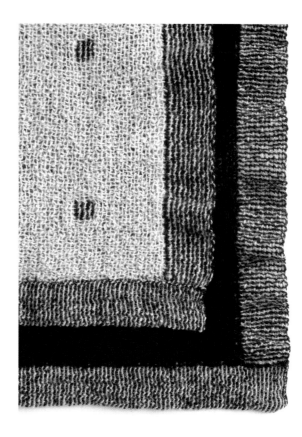

TOP LEFT:

This 'Doublecloth Loop' scarf, with silk warp and crepe wool weft, has natural selvedges for the two cloths. It has been finished with a narrow hem of single cloth in plain weave, using a weft of very fine silk. The hem was machine sewn with a straight stitch while the fabric was still in the loomstate.

TOP RIGHT:

A double cloth, with high-twist wool in both warp and weft, forms the main body of this scarf, while the selvedges are more firmly woven, in single plain weave, giving a slightly rippled effect. The raw edge has also been woven in plain weave, and then turned under to give a hem of roughly similar appearance to the selvedges. A very fine silk weft was used to avoid excessive bulk, and the hem was machine sewn with a zigzag stitch, while the fabric was still in the loomstate.

BOTTOM LEFT:

Hems of various widths and different materials were used to finish the raw edges of these bracelets. (See the Introduction for another view of the bracelets.) Top left: Hem of silver/copper. Bottom left: Copper/polyamide. Right: Silk/steel. Because the warp was silk/steel, it was easy to fold down the hems without having to pin them, as the 'memory' of the metal yarn kept the fabric in place while it was being stitched. The hems were machine sewn with a zigzag stitch, while the fabric was still in the loomstate.

BOTTOM RIGHT:

Over most of its surface this fabric consists of two layers of cloth, one of silk and one of high-twist wool, which weave together at intervals. However, only the silk cloth has been used for the selvedge, giving a gently rippled edge. The raw edge has been finished by weaving a sufficient length of the silk cloth to produce a hem of similar width to the selvedge. The cut edges of the wool cloth are enclosed within this hem, which has been machine sewn with a zigzag stitch, while the fabric was still in the loomstate.

Hemming can be a very successful finish, and may be more in keeping with some items. It is a good idea to use a finer weft for the hem than for the rest of the piece so that, when the fabric has been folded over, the hem does not seem too bulky. Sewing hems on a finished, textured fabric can be a difficult job, so it is much better to do this before wet finishing. Usually it is desirable for the stitching to be as inconspicuous as possible, but although hand stitching is generally very successful in this respect, it is not always essential. The main problem with machine stitching is that standard sewing threads tend to look rather coarse, so it is worth experimenting with fine silk weaving yarns. However, not all sewing machines handle these well, so it is best to try first with a yarn of moderate thickness, such as 60/2 Nm, and then, if this causes no trouble, work your way down gradually to finer yarns. My sewing machine (which is a Bernina) is able to deal with yarns as fine as 40 denier, and this gives an almost invisible line of stitching. As always, the important thing is to experiment with different possibilities at the sampling stage, so that you do not run into unexpected difficulties with a full-size piece.

Building on Experience

Going Beyond Recipes

Many examples of fabrics are shown in this book (in some cases with details of yarns and setts), and these may provide some useful starting points for those who have not worked with high-twist yarns before. However, there have been no 'recipes' in the form of precisely specified projects. Of course, weavers who are new to a particular technique or material may feel a need for some guidance in order to get started. It is natural to feel that a project could ease you into working in this new way. But rigid recipes have their limitations – the analogy with cooking is obvious. As the molecular gastronomist, Hervé This, points out, 'whoever understands the reasons for the results he or she obtains in the kitchen can improve on them.' He contrasts this with the state of being merely a 'hostage to the recipe', when there is no way to rescue the situation if something goes wrong.

In the case of weaving, something that frequently goes wrong is that the original ingredients become unavailable. Yarn manufacturers are depressingly prone to discontinuing interesting yarns. Consequently, books and back numbers of magazines are full of projects requiring yarns that are long gone, and the best that can usually be done in this situation is to search for something of a roughly similar count to use as a substitute. But when working with high-twist yarns, even small changes can give surprisingly different results. And what if you would, in any case, have preferred to use the technique to make something in heavier or finer yarns? By following a strict recipe you are merely relying on someone else's instructions while learning relatively little about why they work. Only by understanding the principles involved can you move on to designing your own fabrics.

Working From Your Records

The best way forward is to develop an understanding of the relationships of yarn, structure and sett that allows you to build on experience. If you keep careful records of everything you do, the information will continue to be of value, even if all the yarns you originally used have since been discontinued. Also, a fabric made when you were a beginner, using relatively coarse yarns, could later be developed into a new design with finer yarns, but using the original information as a starting point. It is also interesting to analyse existing fabrics so that you can learn from them. Structures can be recorded by carefully picking the fabric apart and, though it is less easy to be precise about yarn counts and setts, you can usually learn enough to use as a starting point for your own experiments. In many ways you will find that you use this information intuitively, and there is really no substitute for the tacit knowledge that is built up through such experience. However, there are methods of being more rigorous about transposing information from one situation to another, and they can be very helpful – as Watson remarks about cloth setting, 'theory can be made a very useful adjunct to practice.'

A couple of examples will help to show how the specifications of existing fabrics can be used as a guide when working with different yarns. The first deals with warp-float/weft-float pleating, and the second with crepon fabrics. These examples could also be used as starting points for sampling by anyone who is completely new to these techniques and anxious for some guidance, but if you choose to do this, do not treat them simply as 'projects' to be rigidly followed. The yarns and settings that I describe will get you started, but to get the most out of these examples, you need to move on and experiment with other weft yarns. Cut off your samples frequently and finish them, so that you can get feedback and ideas for what to try next. You could also rethread the reed, to experiment with different setts, and perhaps also try different structures.

Be sure to write down carefully everything you do, to begin to build up records of your own. You could also use the methods outlined here to set up warps with other finer or thicker yarns by calculating appropriate setts in the same way.

Example 1: A New Version of a Pleated Fabric

For many years I have been making variations of a soft pleated fabric using warp-float/weft-float stripes. From studying the many versions of this fabric, it is possible to see that the most successful of them have some things in common in terms of the settings that have been used and the size relationships of the warp and weft yarns. This does not make it possible to derive a 'formula' that will *always* guarantee a good result, but it does provide a useful starting point when working with new yarns.

I have already described some of the important elements required for successful pleating using warp-float/weft-float stripes (*see* Chapter 5). The effect partly results from the relaxation of weft floats as they move from one face of the fabric to the other (though other factors are involved), but this can be achieved in a variety of ways. Also it is possible to produce pleats or ridges in different weights of fabric, suitable for anything from lightweight scarves to jacket fabrics or table linen. My own use of this structure has been mainly for softly draping scarves and lightweight dress fabrics, so my example comes from specifications recorded for fabrics of this type.

Recorded Information as a Starting Point

My records show that the most successful fabrics have had a warp that was thicker (or stiffer) and more closely set (in terms of percentage of maximum sett) than the weft. Also, weft yarns that showed some shrinkage have always greatly assisted the pleating. The less the shrinking potential of the weft, then the greater the discrepancy required, in size or stiffness, between the weft and the warp. However, very high-twist weft yarns have usually not been successful (except when they have also been very much finer than the warp) since they have a tendency to overwhelm the structure rather than co-operating with it. Looking carefully at a variety of fabrics and samples, it becomes possible to be a little more precise about some of these specifications:

▣ Particularly good results were produced with warp setts that were 75–85 per cent of the maximum possible sett, and weft setts that were 37–46 per cent of the maximum sett (these are setts calculated as though each yarn were to be used alone for a balanced twill or Han damask cloth – *see* Chapter 3).

▣ The best results have been when the weft yarn was *substantially* finer than the warp. If the weft yarn was a normal yarn, with no special tendency to shrink, then some degree of pleating began to appear when it was about two thirds of the diameter of the warp, but the best results were achieved when it was much finer than this, preferably close to half the diameter of the warp.

Such relationships between yarns and setts can be used for general guidance when using different yarns, either coarser or finer than those in the original pieces. So, as a rule of thumb, some kind of pleated effect is likely to emerge from any combination of yarns where the warp is about twice the diameter of the weft, and the setts are roughly 80 per cent of maximum for the warp and 40 per cent of maximum for the weft (assuming that stripes of a suitable width are used). This arrangement gives an average sett of about 60 per cent overall. Such a relationship of yarn thickness and density will also give a balanced sett, in the sense of having a similar number of ends and picks/cm (or inch), so producing a stable fabric. This suggests a suitable arrangement for a first sample.

It is very important to recognize that this is *simply a starting point*, and not to assume that it will be perfect. Yarns differ in many ways apart from their thickness, and these other qualities – such as stiffness and smoothness – can only be appreciated by sampling. So it will be wise to weave only a few small samples, perhaps with different wefts that look promising, and then to cut off and finish them, and to get feedback before going any further. It is then possible to start fine-tuning the design, possibly making modifications of sett and yarn, to take account of the particular combination of materials and the intended use of the fabric. This particular rule of thumb relates to the type of lightweight pleated fabrics that I usually produce. Heavier fabrics, for clothing or furnishing, made with the same structure, are likely to work better with very different specifications. The important point is that such relationships can be recorded for *any* type of fabric, so that it

Fabrics using warp-float/weft-float pleating with different combinations of material and structure. *Back*: Wool and silk, in broken twill. *Middle*: Linen and silk, in broken twill and Han damask. *Front*: Silk, with straight twills.

is possible to build on experience and transpose the information to new situations.

Working from a Specific Piece

The 'ideal' sett of 80/40 per cent, given above, provides very general guidance, but many fabrics have been successful with higher or lower setts in warp or weft. Sometimes it will be better to work closely from a specific piece, if this is made from similar fibres or types of yarn as the intended new fabric. Here is an example of an existing piece used in this way.

A pleated sample of silk 60/2 Nm, in 3/1 and 1/3 twill, intended for scarves, has been set at 56 epi, with a weft of silk 210/2 Nm, set at 56 ppi. Ashenhurst's formula (*see* Chapter 3) gives the following information:

Warp yarn = 112 diameters/inch, weft yarn = 210 diameters/inch.

This relationship of yarn diameters, expressed as a percentage: $112/210 \times 100 = 53$

So the diameter of the weft is 53 per cent that of the warp.

(Alternatively this relationship could be described in terms of yardages – the weft is 3.5 times the yardage of the warp.)

The cloth setting formula (*see* Chapter 3) will give the maximum sett for a twill weave, and the actual setts can be expressed as a percentage of this maximum.

Warp sett, 75 per cent of maximum, weft sett: 40 per cent. Average sett: 57.5 per cent.

This information can be used to guide the choice of yarns and setts for a fabric of a lighter or heavier weight. So, let us suppose that silk 30/2 Nm has been chosen as warp, with the aim of making a similar fabric for scarves, but in a heavier weight. The calculations are as follows:

Spun silk 30/2 has 15,000m/kg (converted to imperial measures this gives 7,440yd/lb).

Using Ashenhurst's formula:

The square root of $7,440 = 86.26$
Multiply by 0.92 (as this is a silk yarn)
$86.26 \times 0.92 = 79.36$

Therefore spun silk 30/2 has 79 diameters/inch.

The sett for the new cloth is then worked out as follows:
Maximum sett for 3/1 twill $= \frac{2}{3} \times 79 = 53$
Take 75 per cent of this:
$53 \times 75/100 = 39.75$

The sett closest to this (using imperial reeds) is 40 epi, which gives a suitable starting point for sampling. Working with metric reeds, the closest setting would be 16 ppcm (40.64 epi).

Choosing a Weft

When choosing a weft, the obvious solution is to use the same type of yarn and maintain the same relationship between yarn diameters. At present I have only one spun silk yarn in stock that is roughly the right thickness: 120/2 Nm. This has half the diameter of the warp yarn (and four times the yardage), so it is a little finer in relation to the warp than in the original fabric. A silk yarn of count 100/2 would make a closer match, but it seems preferable to use the yarn I already have, partly because (at the time of writing) both 30/2 Nm and 120/2 Nm yarns are available dyed. Although the preliminary samples will mainly use undyed yarn, it will be useful to find out whether the dyed silk yarns that are readily available work well as a combination.

Aiming for a weft sett of 40 per cent of maximum (as in the original cloth), the spun silk 120/2 should be at 42 ppi. However, although the starting point is to make a fabric of similar quality to the original, it would also be interesting to try different pickings and experiment with other weft yarns, particularly those that are inclined to shrink. I have other yarns in stock that are likely to create some kind of pleating, and perhaps give a rather different hand to the fabric.

Width of Stripes

The width of the stripes is an important consideration in achieving good pleating (*see* Chapter 5), and is a question of the physical size of the pleat as much as the number of threads – a thicker yarn will create a stripe of a certain width with fewer threads than would be required with a fine yarn. However, a thicker yarn will also be able to sustain a wider pleat without sagging, so making this decision is not quite as simple as it looks. Again, looking back at any records of similar fabrics will be helpful.

In this case, the original fabric, with a warp of silk 60/2 set at 56 epi, had stripes of twelve ends, giving a width of 0.214in (0.544cm). As the new yarn is thicker, a first thought is that stripes of fewer ends might be used. But eight ends set at 40 epi would give a stripe 0.2in (0.508cm) wide, and this seems too narrow to give a definite pleat. Twelve ends give a width of 0.3in (0.762cm), slightly wider than the original, which seems about right with this heavier yarn. Sixteen ends would give stripes of 0.4in (1.016cm), which is probably rather wide with such a soft yarn.

Final Specifications of the Warp

Warp: Spun silk 30/2 Nm, 40 epi (4/dent in a 10 dent/in reed or 2/dent in a 20 dent/in reed) 4.5in wide.
3/1 and 1/3 twill stripes of twelve ends.

The Samples

I started by weaving a sample with the spun silk 120/2 Nm as weft, at the calculated sett of 42 ppi, but then tried other pickings of 40, 44 and 48 ppi. I also tried a variety of other weft yarns, including spun silks, including tussah, of several different counts and also some high-twist yarns, in both cotton and wool, calculating setts of 40 per cent for each, to provide a starting point for sampling.

RESULTS

The first sample with 120/2 Nm silk at 42 ppi was successful in producing a fabric of similar characteristics to the original. The other pickings of 40, 44 and 48 ppi all produced satisfactory cloths with good pleating, but varying in firmness. So the original sample, in finer yarn, did provide useful information for planning the new fabric in a heavier weight.

When it came to the other weft yarns, I expected that some of them would be more suitable than others. A tussah yarn, 120/2 Nm, could obviously be expected to work simply because of its fineness, but it was possible that its tendency to shrink would also be helpful. However, though it did create pleats, these were very slightly flattened compared with the more rounded pleats of the cultivated silk. Other, thicker tussah yarns seemed likely to be suitable too, and in practice worked rather better, 70/2 Nm giving a particularly satisfactory pleat. As the tussah yarns have more 'tooth' than the cultivated spun silk, I also tried a slightly lower picking with these yarns.

When it came to the high-twist yarns, some fine cotton crepes (68/1 Nm and 50/1 Nm) seemed likely to be suitable, and this proved to be so. I had anticipated that the wool crepes (27.5/1 Nm and 30/1 Nm) might show a tendency to simply follow their own rhythm, rather than interacting with the structure. This was true for the crepe wool 30/1 Nm, but one of the batches of 27.5/1 Nm (which happens to have a rather soft texture) did create pleating. Further sampling with the crepe 30/1 Nm showed that it could work with the structure if it was more closely picked, but this gave a rather firm cloth quality, not so suitable for scarves (*see* overleaf).

Once you have accomplished your initial aim with a warp like this, it is very worthwhile to go on to experiment with an even wider range of different yarns, and perhaps also different setts of both warp and weft. One idea that particularly interested me was to try some thicker weft yarns, and also to vary the sett of both warp and weft. Some degree of pleating can still be expected when the warp and weft yarns have a closer

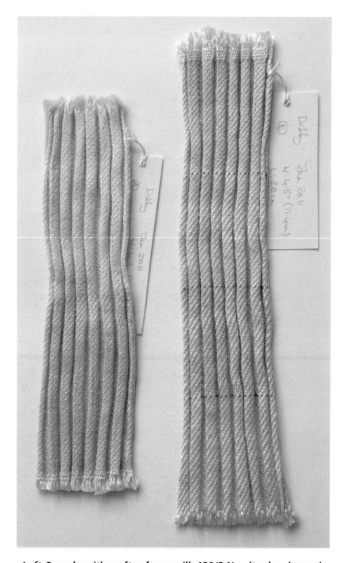

Left: Sample with wefts of spun silk 120/2 Nm *(top)* and tussah 120/2 Nm *(bottom)*, both at 42 ppi. *Right:* Sample comparing tussah wefts, with the picking adjusted so all the wefts are at 38 per cent of maximum sett *(top to bottom)*: 120/2, 40 ppi; 90/2, 35 ppi; 70/2, 30 ppi; 68/2, 30 ppi.

size relationship than I had been using, and perhaps even the warp yarn itself might work as a pleating weft, if sufficiently closely picked, though giving a very different hand to the fabric. The samples show how, with light picking, the pleated effect fades out as the thickness of the weft is increased. In contrast, with a slightly closer warp sett and much heavier weft picking for the thicker yarns, even the 30/2 Nm silk can give some degree of pleating, though it is less tight than with the finer wefts. In both cases, the gradual changes in the width of

Samples showing the effects of different crepe wefts.

Centre: Warp: Spun silk 30/2 Nm, 40 epi. Wefts *(top to bottom)*: Crepe cottons 68/1 Nm, 44 ppi; 50/1 Nm, 40 ppi; 30/1 Nm, 30 ppi. Crepe wool 30/1 Nm, 30 ppi. The crepe cottons all form pleats, but the crepe wool follows its own rhythm.

Left: Warp: Spun silk 30/2 Nm, 40 epi. Weft: Crepe wool 27.5/1 Nm, 28 ppi. The soft-textured yarn *(top)* creates tight pleats, while a similar but slightly stiffer crepe yarn *(bottom)*, from another manufacturer, is a little less successful.

Right: Warp: Spun silk 30/2 Nm, 42 epi. Weft: Crepe wool 30/1 Nm, S *(top)*, 32 ppi, 40 ppi, 48 ppi. Crepe wool Z, *(bottom)*, 48 ppi. The Z twist yarn can be seen to emphasize the Z twill lines in the fabric, since very high-twist yarns break the normal 'rules' of twist-twill interactions (see Chapter 4).

the fabric give a flared shape to the cloth (more examples of fabric shaping are given in Chapter 7).

In a sense this is an easy example, because of the initial aim of producing a fabric comparable to an original piece, and made entirely of normal-twist yarns. In this situation, it is possible to transpose information about yarn relationships and setts with some confidence. Similar types of calculation are widely used in industry, where fabrics of different weight, but of the same fibre and yarn quality, are being produced. On the other hand, extending the experiment by using high-twist yarns across this warp, produced much more variable results. So, although it is always possible to draw upon existing information in this way, sampling becomes even more im-

portant once high-twist yarns, or complex mixtures of yarns, are involved. It is still worth making calculations and using previous experience to plan the first sample, but you must expect more surprises. Crepe yarns from different manufacturers, even when of the same count, may vary a good deal. Unfortunately, even different colours or batches of yarn from a single manufacturer, with the same nominal count and twist specifications, do not always behave in exactly the same way, so it is wise to test new batches of yarn before embarking on a large project. Wetting out small samples of yarn can help you to judge how strongly a particular yarn is likely to react, but in the end, sampling is the only way to be certain what they will do.

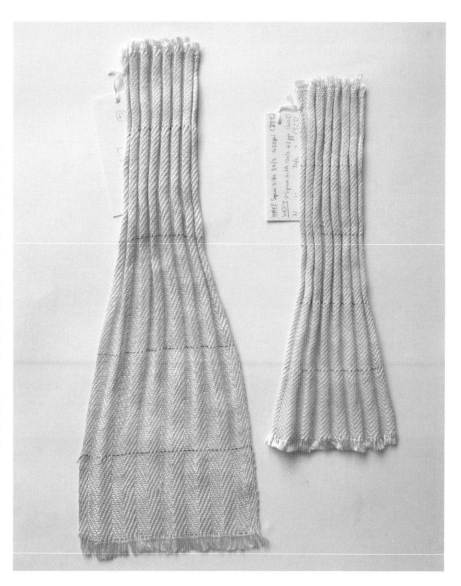

Samples showing fabric shaping with wefts of different thickness. In the left-hand sample the picking is adjusted to keep the *percentage* weft sett roughly similar throughout, while in the right-hand sample, the *picking* has been kept the same and this, of course, means that the percentage weft sett is increasing with the thickness of the yarn.

Left: Warp: Spun silk 30/2 Nm, 40 epi. Weft *(top to bottom)*: Spun silk yarns: 120/2 Nm, 40 ppi (38 per cent); 70/2 Nm, 30 ppi (37 per cent); 60/2 Nm, 28 ppi (37 per cent); 40/2 Nm, 24 ppi (39 per cent); 30/2 Nm, 21 ppi (40 per cent).

Right: Warp: Spun silk 30/2 Nm, 42 epi. Weft *(top to bottom)*: Spun silk yarns: 120/2 Nm, 42 ppi (40 per cent); 70/2 Nm, 42 ppi (52 per cent); 60/2 Nm, 42 ppi (56 per cent); 40/2 Nm, 42 ppi (69 per cent); 30/2 Nm, 42 ppi (79 per cent).

Example 2: Designing Crepons

The difficulties of working with more unpredictable yarns can be illustrated with a second example, the designing of crepon fabrics. Once again, it makes sense to see what has been successful in the past. My records show that setts within a relatively narrow range have given the best results for plain weave crepons. In terms of the overall cloth setting – that is, averaged out between warp and weft – most fabrics have fallen between 43 per cent and 63 per cent of maximum sett. However, the *percentage* settings of warp and weft, and also the relationships of yarn diameters, have been much more variable than in the previous example of warp-float/weft-float pleating. It is possible to produce good crepon effects with a wide range of different combinations of materials and yarn thickness. This variability is partly due to the forcefulness of many high-twist yarns, which are able to create crepons with a wide range of passive yarns of different thickness.

Working with Crepe Wool

Crepe wool 30/1 Nm provides a case in point, since my records show that very different warp and weft setts, and also different yarn relationships, have been equally successful. However, in spite of these differences, the *average* settings for

Successful crepon fabrics can be produced with a variety of different size relationships between the warp and weft.

TOP LEFT:
A Japanese crepon fabric, using a very fine, closely set warp, with a thicker, less closely set weft. (Designer unknown. Ann Sutton Collection)

TOP RIGHT:
In this crepon, the warp has been combined with a much finer weft. Warp: Linen 66 lea, 48 epi. Weft: Crepe silk 60/66 denier, 48 ppi.

BOTTOM LEFT:
A crepon in which both the warp and weft yarns are the same count. Warp: Spun silk 60/2 Nm, 28 epi. Weft: Crepe wool 30/1 Nm, 28 ppi.

BOTTOM RIGHT:
A cotton fabric with warp and weft yarns of roughly similar thickness. Both sets of yarns are unbalanced, but the weft is the more highly twisted of the two. This results in a gentle warpways crepon texture, but faint tracking lines are also visible, since both yarns have the same direction of twist. (Designer unknown)

the different cloths can sometimes be almost the same. For example, this crepe yarn works well as weft, with spun silk 60/2 Nm as a warp, with similar setts for warp and weft, both as epi/ppi and as percentages (30 epi/ppi, giving 54 per cent of maximum sett for both yarns). In contrast, when the same yarn is used with a warp of linen 14 Nm, then the warp and weft settings are similar when given as epi/ppi, but very different as percentages, with 24 epi (62 per cent of maximum), and 24 ppi (44 per cent of maximum). But the settings for this second fabric average out as 53 per cent of maximum sett, almost identical to the cloth with the silk warp.

Crepon Samples with Crepe Wool

Experimenting with crepon makes a very good starting point for sampling for anyone who is new to working with high-twist yarns. As the crepe wool 30/1 Nm is such a versatile yarn, it can be relied on to give good results with many different passive yarns. It is usually best to use it first only as a weft, so that you can become accustomed to handling it before you progress to the more difficult task of using it for warp. So, following the example given above, spun silk 60/2 Nm could be used as warp, set at 28–32 epi (50–57 per cent of maximum

sett) with the crepe yarn as weft at a similar sett. The closest equivalent metric settings would be 11 or 12 epcm (50 or 55 per cent of maximum sett). Alternatively a heavier silk, such as 30/2 Nm, set at 24 epi (60 per cent maximum sett) could be used, with weft setts of 24–28 ppi (44–51 per cent). The closest metric setting is 9 epcm (58 per cent maximum sett), with weft setts of 9–11 ppcm (42–51 per cent). If you have set up a warp for the previous example of warp-float/weft-float pleating, it could also be used for plain weave crepon samples, by rethreading the reed to give this more open sett.

These specifications should be satisfactory as a starting point. But you could then go on to experiment with different weft pickings and other crepe yarns to see how these influence the crepon effect. Cut off and finish samples frequently to get feedback. Once you have produced some good crepon textures, other possibilities could be explored, such as alternating the crepe yarn with passive yarns to give seersucker stripes, or rethreading the reed to give a different sett or a crammed and spaced arrangement (*see* Chapter 4).

Going Beyond Crepon

Although I have suggested these warp yarns and settings as suitable for plain weave crepons, they will also work well for other techniques. While you have such a warp on the loom, you could also choose to experiment with various weave structures, depending on the threading you have chosen. For example, with an eight-shaft straight draft, both waffle and lace weaves could be tried. When woven with high-twist yarns and contrasted with plain weave in normal yarns, these structures produce good seersucker effects (*see* Chapter 5). The cloth settings that I have suggested would also be suitable for warp-float/weft-float pleats, but woven sideways, requiring only four shafts (*see* Chapter 5). In this case the *weft* would need to be substantially thicker or stiffer than the warp – the calculation methods shown in the previous example can be used as a guide in choosing wefts.

Crepe Yarn as Warp

Once you have become used to handling the crepe yarn as weft, you could try making a warp with it, choosing a sett on the basis of information from your samples on the first warp (*see* Chapter 8 for advice about warping with high-twist yarns). A wide variety of passive yarns could then be tried as weft, to produce crossways crepon pleating. Such a warp will also be suitable for working with crepe yarns in the weft, exploring the different textures that can be produced from same-twist and opposite-twist yarns (*see* Chapter 4). Keep careful records of everything you do. Of course, all yarns are subject to being discontinued, and if you cannot obtain any of the suggested yarns, then try substituting others, but using roughly similar percentages as recommended above, to calculate an appropriate sett to use as a starting point.

Matching Active and Passive Yarns

Although worsted-spun crepe yarns, such as crepe wool 30/1 Nm, tend to be particularly versatile, do not assume that all high-twist yarns will produce crepon effects with passive yarns of *any* thickness or stiffness. For each yarn there will be limits to the range of possible 'partners' that are likely to prove successful. It is important to pay attention to the physical properties of both normal and high-twist yarns, because variations in twist and stiffness can cause apparently similar yarns to behave in very different ways. Throughout this book, examples have been given of the variable nature of high-twist yarns. Some form a small-scale crinkled texture, while others tend to form larger-scale spirals as they move through the cloth. These characteristics determine whether a particular yarn will be able to create a crepon texture only with passive yarns that are a similar thickness or finer than itself, or whether it can also pleat yarns that are much thicker.

Variations in twist and stiffness influence both the amplitude (width) and pitch (tightness) of the spirals that high-twist yarns can form. For example, a stiff, slightly unbalanced mohair yarn, 22 wc (24.8 Nm), which spirals with a very large amplitude but shallow pitch, is excellent for forming a large-scale pleated effect in an open gauze weave. However, it lacks the energy to create a crepon in a more closely woven fabric. In contrast, slightly less stiff, but more energetic yarns (such as the crepe wools) will form spirals of slightly smaller amplitude but with a much steeper pitch, and this explains why these are such excellent yarns for producing crepons in plain weave with passive yarns of various thickness. But, compared with the mohair, these yarns are less effective at creating distinct pleating in a gauze weave, since they are inclined to form small curls and kinks between the warp threads, leaving less energy available to disturb the surface of the fabric.

A softer, woollen-spun yarn, such as the merino 14.5 Nm, will tend to form a spiral of relatively small amplitude *in relation to its thickness*, though still with a steep pitch due to its

high levels of twist. A yarn of this type is likely to be less successful at forming crepons with yarns that are much thicker than itself, though it can work very well with finer yarns. It is also excellent in float weaves, where its tight spirals give good shrinkage. These different forms of spiral also have implications for the ways in which high-twist yarns are likely to interact with one another.

Of course, these comparisons drastically simplify and idealize the situation, since wide variations of amplitude and pitch will arise with the many different possible combinations of fibre, spinning technique, yarn thickness and twist angle. But even such a simple approach can be helpful in trying to understand how high-twist yarns work and in making judgements about the best ways of using them. By asking yourself what kind of spiral you would *expect* a yarn to make, depending on characteristics such as thickness, stiffness and twist, you can get some idea of whether it is likely to work well for crisp surface textures, such as crepons, or will be better suited to float weaves requiring good shrinkage. However, as with all theorizing, this can only be a starting point that must be tested by experiment. Remember – theory is all very well, but it doesn't stop things happening!

Reflection and Experiment

My aim in writing this book has been to share my personal experience and also the knowledge I have gained from other people. This is, of course, a work in progress. In many places I have made suggestions about what I *think* may be going on, and have expressed my present opinion about the best way to approach a particular design problem or technique. But, given the variable nature of materials and structures, and especially the unpredictability of high-twist yarns, there will always be uncertainties where more research is needed. I hope that readers will be inspired to join in what Lotte Dalgaard has called 'the continuing experiment', to try and solve some of the many remaining puzzles. Inevitably, with so many subtle factors interacting, it is not always easy to understand what is happening and why. Hippocrates had the same trouble with medicine: 'Life is short, the art is long, opportunity fleeting, experience misleading, judgement difficult.' So it is important to adopt an open-minded experimental approach, carefully noting results, reflecting on what they mean, and letting one experiment lead to the next. In this way, the design process can go forward as an interplay between your design ideas and the possibilities of materials and structures.

Gauze fabrics with different wefts. *Left:* A stiff mohair yarn forms spirals of high amplitude but low pitch, creating large scale pleating. *Right:* A crepe wool yarn forms spirals of smaller amplitude but higher pitch. The yarn has a tendency to form small kinks between the openly set warp yarns, leaving less energy available to disturb the surface of the fabric.

'Triple Spiral' neckpiece. A very fine silk crepe yarn forms a spiral of small amplitude and very high pitch, giving an excellent shrinkage of floats in this pleated structure. Silk, steel, crepe silk and polyester reflective yarn.

BIBLIOGRAPHY

The bibliography contains books and articles that I have referred to in the text, and others that include useful information about spinning and weaving, or examples of strongly textured fabrics. Details are also included of books that give good accounts of weave structure, including industrial texts. Some of these are now out of print but are well worth searching for.

Albers, Anni, *On Designing* (Wesleyan University Press, 1961)

Albers, Anni, *On Weaving* (Wesleyan University Press, 1965)

Alderman, Sharon, 'Tracking the Mystery of the Crinkling Cloth', *Handwoven* (Sept/Oct 1985, pp. 31–33)

Alderman, Sharon, *Mastering Weave Structures* (Interweave Press, 2004)

Arn-Grischott, Ursina, *Doubleweave on Four to Eight Shafts* (Interweave Press, 1999)

Barrett, Clotilde and Smith, Eunice, *Double Two-Tie Unit Weaves* (Weaver's Journal Publications, 1983)

Behn, Dörte, 'Intelligent Textiles – The Originals', *Textile Forum* (3, 2009, p. 1)

Buchanan, Rita, 'Measuring Yarn. Part 3: Twist', *Spin-Off* (Winter 1993, pp. 56–60)

Burnham, Dorothy, K., *Cut My Cote* (The Royal Ontario Museum, 1973)

Champeney, Anna, 'Fun with Floats: Crinkle Scarves with Classic Overshot', *The Journal for Weavers, Spinners and Dyers* (232, Winter 2009, pp. 21–23)

Champeney, Anna, 'Weaver Profile: Lotte Dalgaard', The Journal for Weavers, Spinners and Dyers (236, Winter 2010, pp. 7–9)

Clarke, Amy, C., 'Organic Structure: The Art of Overtwist with Ann Richards' *Handwoven* (Nov/Dec 1996, pp. 32–34)

Cochrane, Grace, *Liz Williamson: Textiles (*Craftsman House, 2008)

Colchester, Chloë, *The New Textiles* (Thames & Hudson, 1991)

Collingwood, Peter, *Textile and Weaving Structures* (Batsford, 1987)

Cross, Dorothy, 'Plain Weave with a Twist or Two!', *Handwoven* (Jan/Feb, 2003, pp. 44–47)

Dalgaard, Lotte, *Magiske materiale – i væven (Magical materials – in weaving)* (FiberFeber, 2007) (In Danish with English translation on CD)

Dalgaard, Lotte, *Magical Materials to Weave* (Trafalgar: in press)

Durant, Judith (ed.), *Handwoven Scarves* (Interweave Press, 1999)

Ellen, Alison, *Knitting: colour, structure and design* (The Crowood Press, 2011)

Elliott, Lillian, 'In Search of Collapse', *In Celebration of the Curious Mind* (Interweave Press, 1983, pp. 103–109)

Emery, Irene, *The Primary Structures of Fabrics* (The Textile Museum, 1980)

Field, Anne, *Collapse Weave* (A&C Black, 2008)

Frame, Mary, 'Ringlets and Waves: Undulations from Overtwist', *Spin-Off* (December 1986, pp. 28–33)

Frame, Mary, 'Are You Ready to Collapse?', *Spin-Off* (March 1987, pp. 41–46)

Frame, Mary, 'Save the Twist: Warping and Weaving with Overtwisted Yarns', *Spin-Off* (June 1987, pp. 43–48)

Gordon, J. E., *Structures* (Penguin Books, 1978)

Hald, Margrethe, *Ancient Danish Textiles from Bogs and Burials* (The National Museum of Denmark, 1980)

Hall, Rosalind, *Egyptian Textiles* (Shire Publications, 1986)

Hall, Rosalind, 'Crimpled" Garments: a mode of Dinner Dress', *Discussions in Egyptology* (5, 1986, pp. 37–45)

Hallman, Eileen, 'Crepe and Shape', *Spin-Off* (Fall 1999, pp. 77–79)

Harvey-Brown, Stacey, *Woven Shibori for Textural Effects* (The Loom Room Publications, 2010)

Harvey-Brown, Stacey, *Honeycomb for Textural Effects* (The Loom Room Publications, 2011)

Harvey-Brown, Stacey, *Beneath the Surface* (The Loom Room Publications, 2011)

Hertel, Heinrich, *Structure, Form, Movement* (Reinhold Publishing Corporation, 1966)

Hochberg, Bette, 'Add a New Twist to Your Spinning', *Spin-Off* (1981, pp. 42–45)

Ignell, Tina, 'The Technician with a Flair for Design', *Vävmagasinet: Scandinavian Weaving Magazine* (1/04, pp. 10–15) (Article about Andreas Möller)

Ignell, Tina, 'Sculptural Textiles and Sacred Weaves', *Vävmagasinet: Scandinavian Weaving Magazine* (4/06, pp. 6–8) (Article about Lotte Dalgaard)

Jackson, Paul, *Folding Techniques for Designers: From Sheet to Form* (Laurence King Publishing, 2011)

Kemp, Barry, J. and Vogelsang-Eastwood, Gillian, *The Ancient Textile Industry at Amarna* (Egypt Exploration Society, 2001)

Leitner, Christina, *Paper Textiles*, (A&C Black, 2005)

Masterson, Vicki, 'Texture with Deflected Double Weave', *Fabrics That Go Bump*, Madelyn van der Hoogt (ed.), (XRS Books, 2002, pp. 103–5)

McCarthy, Cara and McQuaid, Matilda, *Structure and Surface: Contemporary Japanese Textiles* (The Museum of Modern Art, 1998)

Millar, Lesley (ed.), *21 21: the textile vision of Reiko Sudo and Nuno* (University College for the Creative Arts, 2005)

Morris, Wendy, 'Work in Progress – Research into Wires and Metallics', *Complex Weavers Journal* (Feb 2010, pp. 36–39)

Nisbet, Harry, *Grammar of Textile Design* (Scott, Greenwood & Son, 1906)

Nuno Corporation, *Fuwa Fuwa* (Nuno Corporation, 1998)

Nuno Corporation, *Boro Boro* (Nuno Corporation, 1998)

Oelsner, G.H., *A Handbook of Weaves* (Dover Publications, 1952, unaltered republication of original edition of 1915)

Osterkamp, Peggy, *Warping Your Loom and Tying On New Warps* (Lease Sticks Press, 1997)

Osterkamp, Peggy, *Weaving for Beginners – An Illustrated Guide* (Lease Sticks Press, 2010)

Quinn, Celia, 'Experimenting with silk crepe', *Spin-Off* (December 1986, pp. 36–37)

Reimann, Peter, 'Firing the Creative Urge: Sheila Reimann – Handweaver', *Creative Fibre* (September 2007, vol. 10, no. 2, pp. 14–16)

Richards, Ann, 'Ann Richards – handweaver and designer from England' *Vävmagasinet: Scandinavian Weaving Magazine* (No. 4, 1990, pp. 14–15)

Richards, Ann, 'Abracadabra' ('Pleat effect' scarf design) *Vävmagasinet: Scandinavian Weaving Magazine* (No. 4, 1990, pp. 16–17)

Richards, Ann, 'Breaking into Waves', *Handwoven* (Nov/Dec 1996, pp. 35–38)

Richards, Ann, 'Designing with Crepons', *Weavers* (Spring 1999, Vol. 11, No. 3, pp. 24–27)

Richards, Ann, 'Form as Formation in Nature and Design: "A Diagram of Forces"', *Textile Forum* (1, 2003, pp. 36–39)

Richards, Ann, 'Wonderful Yarns from Copenhagen', *The Journal for Weavers, Spinners and Dyers* (222, June 2007, pp. 26–28)

Riley, Bridget, *Mondrian: Nature to Abstraction* (Tate Gallery Publishing, 1997)

Robinson, A.T.C. and Marks, R., *Woven Cloth Construction* (The Textile Institute, 1973)

Ross, Mabel, *The Essentials of Yarn Design for Handspinners* (Mabel Ross, 1983)

Schoeser, Mary, *International Textile Design* (Laurence King 1995)

Schön, Donald, A., *The Reflective Practitioner* (Avebury, 1991)

Straub, Marianne, *Hand Weaving and Cloth Design* (The Viking Press, 1977)

Strong, John, H., *Foundations of Fabric Structure* (National Trade Press, 1946)

Sutton, Ann, *The Structure of Weaving* (Hutchinson, 1982)

Sutton, Ann, Collingwood, Peter, and St Aubyn Hubbard, Geraldine, *The Craft of the Weaver* (BBC, 1982)

Sutton, Ann, and Sheehan, Diane, *Ideas in Weaving* (Batsford, 1989)

Sutton, Ann, 'The Textiles of Junichi Arai, Hon RDI', *The Journal for Weavers, Spinners and Dyers* (161, March 1992, pp. 14–15)

Teal, Peter, *Hand Woolcombing and Spinning* (Blandford Press, 1976)

Truslow, N. A., *A Handbook of Twisting* (Clarke Publishing Company, 1957)

van der Hoogt, Madelyn, *et al.*, 'A Perplexing Plethora of Pleats', *Fabrics That Go Bump*, Madelyn van der Hoogt (ed.), (XRS Books, 2002, pp. 103–5)

van der Hoogt, Madelyn, *The Complete Book of Drafting for Handweavers* (Unicorn Books, 2010)

Watson, William, *Textile Design and Colour (6th Edition)* (Longmans, 1954)

Watson, William, *Advanced Textile Design (2nd Edition)* (Longmans, 1925)

Whiting, David, *Deirdre Wood: straight and narrow* (University College for the Creative Arts, 2005)

Williamson, Liz, 'Fulled Seersucker Scarves', *Fabrics That Go Bump*, Madeyn van der Hoogt (ed.), (XRS Books, 2002, pp. 103–5)

USEFUL ADDRESSES
AND WEBSITES

Sharon Alderman
www.sharonalderman.com

Junichi Arai
1-1228, Sakaino, Kiryu, 376-0002, Japan
email: jun-ichi@ktv.ne.jp

Dörte Behn
www.doerte_behn.de

Anna Champeney
www.annachampeney.com

Fiona Crestani
f.crestani@sbg.at

Lotte Dalgaard
lotte.dalgaard@pc.dk

Alison Ellen
www.alisonellenhandknits.co.uk

Berthe Forchhammer
www.wwweave.dk
www.vaevevaerkstedet.dk

Mary Frame
framem@hotmail.com

Stacey Harvey-Brown
www.theloomroom.co.uk

Teresa Kennard
www.purecolordrama.com

Bobbie Kociejowski
www.bobbiekociejowski.com

Gilian Little
gilian.little@virgin.net

Noriko Matsumoto
www7b.biglobe.ne.jp/~norikomatsumoto/

Andreas Möller
www.moeller-hamburg.com

Wendy Morris
wendy@wendymorris.co.uk

Nuno
www.nuno.com

Jennie Parry
21 St Philip's Road, Leicester LE5 5TR, UK
+44 (0) 1162 737189

Ann Richards
16 Albany Road, Southsea, PO5 2AB, UK
acostall@yahoo.com
www.caa.org.uk
www.craftscouncil.org.uk/photostore

Lucia Schwalenberg
www.lucia-schwalenberg-weberei.de

Emma Sewell
www.wallacesewell.com

Geraldine St Aubyn Hubbard
Rosebrook, Farm Lane, Nutbourne, Chichester,
W. Sussex, PO18 8SA, UK
+44 (0) 1243 377372

Ann Sutton
www.annsutton.info
asutton@macdream.net

Växbo Lin
www.vaxbolin.se

Liz Williamson
lizwilliamson.com.au
www.cofa.unsw.edu.au/about-us/staff/30
liz.williamson@unsw.edu.au
Liz Williamson, Head,
School of Design Studies, College of Fine Arts,
University of New South Wales, PO Box 259,
Paddington, NSW 2021, Australia

Deirdre Wood
woodwarp@hotmail.co.uk

SUPPLIERS

Don Porrit Looms
The Studio, Leathley Road, Menston, Ilkley,
W. Yorks, LS29 6DPT
Tel: 01943 878329
Fax: 01943 884141
Extremely helpful supplier of looms and equipment (including autodenters).

Eurestex
(Contact: Richards Cockcroft)
Park View Mills, Raymond Street, Bradford, BD5 8DT
Tel: 01274 721231
Fax: 01274 390903
info@eurestex.co.uk
www.eurestex.co.uk
A very good source of silk yarns in various weights, including dyed spun silk 60/2 and 120/2 Nm.

George Weil & Sons, Ltd
Old Portsmouth Road, Peasmarsh, Guildford,
Surrey, GU3 1LZ
Tel: 01483 565800
Fax: 01483 565807
esales@georgeweil.com
www.georgeweil.com
High-twist botany wool yarn 2/36 wc,18 tpi and 30 tpi, and balanced yarn of the same count.
High-twist silk yarn, 4 x 40/44 denier, S and Z.
A variety of standard yarns, including dyed spun (shantung) yarn 60/2 Nm.
Looms and equipment, including end-delivery hand shuttles and autodenters.

The Danish Yarn Purchasing Association (GIF)
To buy yarns from the Association you have to be a member. Yarns can only be bought from the webshop.
www.yarn.dk
info@yarn.dk
A wide variety of unusual yarns, including a good selection of industrial crepe yarns.

Habu Textiles
135 West 29th Street, Suite 804, New Yarn City,
NY 10001, USA
Tel: 212 239 3546
Fax: 212 239 4173
habu@habutextiles.com
www.habutextiles.com
A wide variety of unusual yarns, including metal/textile blends and wool and silk crepe yarns from Japan.

The Handweavers Studio and Gallery
140 Seven Sisters Road, London N7 7N
Tel: 020 7272 1891
Fax: 020 7272 4649
info@handweavers.co.uk
www.handweavers.co.uk
A very extensive selection of yarns, both standard and specialist, including metal/textile blends, synthetic shrink yarns and high-twist yarns, including Japanese industrial crepe yarns and woollen merino 14.5 Nm.
Looms and equipment, including end-delivery hand shuttles.

INDEX